How to Be Yourself

300 Inspirational Quotes
A Guide to Living an Authentic Life

Edited with commentary
by Michael Nagel

Michael Nagel LLC
Portland, Oregon 2015

How to Be Yourself

Copyright © 2015 Michael Nagel.

Published by Michael Nagel LLC

ISBN 978-0-9849961-1-7

CONTENTS

Part Two: Becoming Your Self

PREFACE

I wish I had the courage to live life true to myself, not the life others expected of me.

~ the number one regret of dying persons
as reported by palliative nurse Bronnie Ware
in *The Top Five Regrets of the Dying*

Few things in life are more important than learning how to be yourself. Unfortunately teachings about authenticity and encouragements to be your own person are just as few.

This book is an exception. If you want to learn how to be yourself, this book is for you.

If amid the pressures to conform and to be just like everyone else you need encouragement to stay true to yourself, this book is for you.

How to Be Yourself shares more than 300 inspirational quotes and excerpts related to your living an authentic life. They are from psychological and spiritual paths for development as well as from literature, poetry, film, song, cartoon, and philosophy. Organized into 12 chapters, the quotes help you to understand many of the issues you face and the skills you need to create a life that is true to yourself.

Some quotes are short and memorable, some others are paragraph-length explorations of important points. All of them express the wisdom that others have left behind to mark the path home to yourself.

These inspiring quotations have brought clarity and encouragement to my clients with whom I work in private practice as a therapist and an authenticity coach and to participants in my workshops.

The quotes could be thought to integrate two poles of the spectrum of experience: existential and spiritual. The existential concerns how we as everyday persons typically experience and reconcile ourselves to the limiting facts of our human existence such as our being responsible for the lives we make for ourselves.

The spiritual concerns the vast potential of human nature, believed in by many, but experienced personally by relatively few. Understandably scientific materialism gives many persons good reason to doubt the existence of the spiritual dimension of life, but that is like saying Mars does not exist because you have not been there yourself.

Existentialism and spirituality - each is a true perspective depending upon one's realization. When integrated, these two perspectives present a more complete view of the quest for personal authenticity.

Accordingly, the book is divided into two parts related to these two dimensions of the quest for authenticity: Becoming Your Own Person and Becoming Your Self.

When you choose to live your own authentic life, you enter upon the mythical hero's journey. The journey involves facing issues and learning skills which are addressed in the first 10 chapters of inspirational quotes. The last two chapters address what I call the "deep authenticity" of becoming your Self. A brief commentary introduces each chapter..

Following are brief descriptions of what you can look forward to learning in the twelve chapters into which the book is divided. As shown in the table of contents, some chapters are subdivided into sections for your more precise understanding.

The Call to an Authentic Life – In this section you will learn how the mental and emotional pain from which we sometimes suffer calls us from inauthentic living to a life of fulfillment.

Entering the Wilderness – Responding to this call requires separating from others, turning your back on conformity, and entering the wilderness of your undiscovered self.

Uniqueness and Individuality – You are unique, one of a kind. Yet life beckons you to actualize your uniqueness by becoming an individual.

Personal Autonomy – Where conformity directs you to listen to others for direction, being your own person requires that you rely upon yourself for direction and guidance.

The Question of Morality — At some time on your journey, your self-direction may come into apparent conflict with moral standards. Where do standards of right and wrong come from? Is there a deeper "truth" with which autonomy does not conflict?

Psychological Wholeness — To be yourself, be all that you are, not just the bright and shiny part into which we sometimes divide ourselves.

The Question of Beliefs — Beliefs about what is true bring you the comfort of certainty about things you have never experienced for yourself. But is this authentic? Instead of belief can you have the courage to doubt and the will to find out for yourself what truth may be?

Psychological Agency — While birth gives you uniqueness, your birthing your own individuality requires that you labor with the powers of freedom, choice, will, action, and personal responsibility.

Living in Process — Whenever did you not experience change? You are not a fixed "thing", but a dynamic, unfolding, process of becoming.

Approaches to Transformation — How do you change to become more authentic? Not by squeezing yourself into ideals imagined by others! How could patterning yourself after an outer ideal lead you closer to your inner self? There is another way.

The Veil of Thought — You are not your thoughts. Deep authenticity guides you to understand that while thought is a useful tool for functioning, thought hides your deeper Self.

The Self — Beyond the customary way of understanding the self, the Self of deep authenticity ultimately fulfills the quest for authenticity. It is the source from which your call to an authentic life first sounded.

If these topics resonate with you, then yes this book is for you.

No better time exists to start your journey to yourself than now.

.

Michael Nagel
Vancouver Washington, June 2015

How to Use This Book

Take pleasure in reading *How to Be Yourself* from beginning to end or in any order you wish. As much as possible, the quotes within a chapter are arranged as a flow of related ideas.

Let me suggest that you take the time to read slowly, savor, and digest the wisdom gleaned from the life experience of these remarkable persons of the past and present.

Out of respect, I have not changed the quotes' original gender references, i.e. him/her. Of course, wisdom applies to all persons.

I designed the book to be *more useful and educational* than inspirational quotes books which provide only the quote and the name of the person to whom the quote is attributed. Here for each quote you will also find:

Some flesh and bones – Where known you will find not only by the person to whom the quote is attributed, but also when that person lived, his/her country of origin, 'profession', and the source from which the quote is derived.

In addition, you will also find for your benefit:

Author index – Some quotes will become favorites, and you may want to revisit them again and again. Others you may want to share with friends. The Author Index helps you to find those quotes with ease.

Glossary – Where an unfamiliar term first appears in the book, it is made **bold**, and defined in the glossary.

Bibliography – If you feel inspired to read more, here you will find the information needed to buy or borrow.

Finally, I have made every effort to verify the accuracy of the quotations by my verifying the quotation in the source when that source has been available. Any errors that may exist are solely my responsibility.

Enjoy!

Part One:

Becoming Your Own Person

1

THE CALL TO AN AUTHENTIC LIFE

These pains that you feel are messengers.
Listen to them. Turn them to sweetness.

~ Jalal ad-Din Muhammad Rumi
Persian poet and **Sufi** master
"A Man and a Woman Arguing" in *The Essential Rumi*
translated by Coleman Barks

Typically we turn away from unpleasant feelings rather than turn towards them. We run from the daytime anxiety that shadows our every footstep. We drown our sorrow in beer and wine. We reach for sleeping pills to quiet the deep questions that keep us awake at night.

You might question, what good could possibly come from tending to such troublesome feelings? Or as a client once asked me about painful feelings, "Why would I want to go there?" Yet just as bodily pain signals something is wrong, so too does the soul's pain.

When you ignore the body's signals, you do so at our peril. Similarly you endanger yourself when you ignore your soul's pains.

Distress often results from living in a way which is not true to yourself. You betray yourself when you live according to the desires, goals and values of others such as your parents, teachers, friends, partners, and society. It's as if you vacate your own life. However you do so at a very real personal cost.

Palliative nurse Bronnie Ware reports in her book, *The Top Five Regrets of the Dying*, that the number one regret of dying persons is, "I wish I had the courage to live life true to myself, not the life others expected of me." Such regret results from ignoring your soul's pain. You don't want to end our life with such regret.

Rather than running from or numbing yourself, instead hear your soul's pain as a call from your depths. It calls you to a more authentic life. If you heed that call, you begin an adventure in self-discovery which some call the hero's journey.

◊ ◊ ◊

The call at the beginning is a vague, almost imperceptible and mysterious flame. It shows itself as a questioning of the disharmony you live in. It is your disharmony, as you experience it. It is your own questioning. And it is your personal yearning.

~ A. H. Almaas (1944-present)
Kuwaiti-born American psychologist and philosopher
in *Essence: The Diamond Approach to Inner Realization*

It is tragic how few people ever 'possess their souls' before they die.... Most people are other people. Their thoughts are someone else's opinions, their lives a mimicry, their passions a quotation.

~ Oscar Wilde (1854-1900)
Irish playwright, novelist, and poet
in *De Profundis*

My life had got on the wrong track, and my contact with men had become now a mere soliloquy. I had fallen so low that, if I had to choose between falling in love with a woman and reading a book about love, I should have chosen the book.

~ The narrator in *Zorba the Greek*,
by Nikos Kazantzakis (1883–1957)
Greek author, poet, and philosopher

Haller's sickness of the soul, as I now know, is not the eccentricity of a single individual, but the sickness of the times themselves, the neurosis of that generation to which Haller belongs, a sickness, it seems, that by no means attacks the weak and worthless only but, rather, precisely those who are strongest in spirit and richest in gifts.

~ The narrator, in *Steppenwolf*
by Herman Hesse (1877-1962)
German author

I have of late, but wherefore I know not, lost all my mirth, forgone all custom of exercises, and, indeed, it goes so heavily with my disposition that this goodly frame, the earth, seems to me a sterile promontory; this most excellent canopy, the air, look you, this brave o'erhanging firmament, this majestical roof fretted with golden fire, - why, it appeareth nothing to me but a foul and pestilent congregation of vapors.

~ The character of Hamlet in *Hamlet*,
by William Shakespeare (1564-1616)
English playwright

When I was young, it seemed that life was so wonderful, a miracle,
Oh it was beautiful, magical.
And all the birds in the trees, they'd be singing so happily,
Oh joyfully, oh playfully, watching me.
But then they sent me away, to teach me how to be sensible,
Logical, oh responsible, practical.
And they showed me a world where I could be so dependable
Oh clinical, oh intellectual, cynical.

There are times when all the world's asleep,
The questions run too deep for such a simple man.
Won't you please, please tell me what went wrong.
I know it sounds absurd.
Please tell me who I am.

~ Roger Hodgson (1950-present)
English writer and composer
in the song *The Logical Song*

I discovered that I was drifting without rudder or compass, swept in all directions by influence from custom, tradition, fashion, swayed by standards uncritically accepted from my friends, my family, my countrymen, my ancestors. Were these reliable guides for one's life? I could not assume that they were, for everywhere around me I saw old ways of doing things breaking down and proving inadequate... But what else was there? If I was neither to do simply what other people did, nor just what was expected of me, what guide was there?

~ Joanna Field (1900-1998)
English author
in *A Life of One's Own*

... Her dilemma is simply a caricature of the dilemma we all have encountered, an identification with our adaptations, a confusion of the Self with our persona. Sooner or later, a great distress will rise from our soul to trouble us, perplex us, dismay us, but which, if we can possibly query it to find what it wants from us, will prove to be our best friend.

~ James Hollis Ph.D. (1940-present)
American **Jungian analyst** and author
in *What Matters Most*

The mass of men lead lives of quiet desperation. What is called resignation is confirmed desperation. From the desperate city you go into the desperate country, and have to console yourself with the bravery of minks and muskrats.

~ Henry David Thoreau (1817-1862)
American **transcendentalist** naturalist, and author
in *Walden*

The context of the general teachings is one of talking to a sentient being who is experiencing uninterrupted bewilderment – one thought or emotion after another like the surface of the ocean in turmoil, without any recognition of mind essence. This confusion is continuous, without almost any break, life after life.

~ Tulku Urgyen Rinpoche (1920-1995)
Tibetan Buddhist **Dzogchen** Master
in *As It Is, Vol. II*

Others can give you a name or a number, but they can never tell you who you really are. That is something you yourself can only discover from within.

~ Thomas Merton (1915–1968)
American Trappist monk, writer, and mystic
in *No Man is an Island*

Bagger Vance: Yep ... Inside each and every one of us is one true authentic swing... Somethin' we was born with... Somethin' that's ours and ours alone... Somethin' that can't be taught to ya or learned... Somethin' that got to be remembered ... Over time the world can, rob us of that swing ... It get buried inside us under all our wouldas and couldas and shouldas ... Some folk even forget what their swing was like ...

~ the character, Bagger Vance in the movie *Bagger Vance*
screenplay by Jeremy Leven

There is something in every one of you that waits and listens for the sound of the genuine in yourself. It is the only true guide you will ever have. And if you cannot hear it, you will all of your life spend your days on the ends of strings that somebody else pulls.

~ Howard Thurman (1899-1981)
African American author, theologian, educator, and civil rights leader

In the final analysis, we count for something only because of the essential we embody, and if we do not embody that, life is wasted...

~ Carl Jung (1875-1961)
Swiss depth psychologist
in *Memories, Dreams, Reflections*

O air-borne voice! long since, severely clear,
A cry like thine in my own heart I hear:
"Resolve to be thyself; and know that he,
Who finds himself, loses his misery!"

~ Matthew Arnold (1822-1888)
English poet
in *Self Dependence*

And the day came when the risk to remain tight in a bud was more painful than the risk it took to blossom.

~ Anais Nin (1903-1977)
French-Cuban author and diarist

2

ENTERING THE WILDERNESS

In the later stages of what I had thought was a lonely trail I came upon the outskirts of a country which seemed to be well known to the few, though little spoken of and I think unguessed at by the many.

~ Joanna Field (1900-1998)
English author
in *A Life of One's Own*

Imagine yourself about to enter a wilderness. Before you a trail leads into the unknown. Having left civilization behind, you stand totally alone. No one will guide you. Dangers may lurk. You have only yourself to reply upon.

So too you are alone when entering the wilderness of your undiscovered self.

Leaving behind the city of conventional values and expectations, you break with property, status, and credentials as the criteria of the good life. The measure of a bank balance accounts for little compared to the measure of your soul.

Whether or not friends approve matters not, for you have heeded your call to be an individual. Before you the trail into the wilderness seems sparse. Few have trodden it. Yet some have left markers.

The trials of your self-exile will be real. You will have to shelter yourself from the criticisms of others. You will learn to nourish yourself from within and to be good company to yourself. You will start the fire of your own understanding, and become a lamp unto yourself that illumines the values, inclinations, and wonders of your own unique nature.

We do not receive wisdom, we must discover it for ourselves, after a journey through the wilderness, which no one else can make for us, which no one can spare us, for our wisdom is the point of view from which we come at last to regard the world.

~ Marcel Proust (1871-1922)
French novelist

Conscientious - so call I him who goeth into god-forsaken wildernesses, and hath broken his venerating heart ...
Free from the happiness of slaves, redeemed from deities and adorations, fearless and fear-inspiring, grand and lonesome: so is the will of the conscientious.
In the wilderness have ever dwelt the conscientious, the free spirits as lords of the wilderness; but in the cities dwell the well-foddered, famous wise ones - the draught beasts.

~ The character of Zarathustra in *Thus Spake Zarathustra*
by Friedrich Nietzsche (1844-1900)
German philosopher

On one or on several occasions in the course of their lives, even the most harmless people do not altogether escape coming into conflict with the fine virtues of piety and gratitude. Sooner or later each of us must take the step that separates him from his father, from his mentors; each of us must have some cruelly lonely experience--even if most people cannot take much of this and soon crawl back.

~ The character of Demian, in *Demian*
by Herman Hesse (1877-1962)
German author

It is in vain to dream of a wildness distant from ourselves. There is none such. [*Journal*, 30 August 1856]

~ Henry David Thoreau (1817-1862)
American transcendentalist, naturalist, and author
in *The Journal of Henry David Thoreau 1837-1861*

To individuate you must go your own way in life, breaking free of the social pressures and beliefs that keep you from being who you are, going off, symbolically speaking, into the dark forest or into the wilderness, finding your own unique path, thereby becoming a true individual. You must be liberated from the womb of culture and from the conditioned ego-personality and persona it supports.

~ Keiron Le Grice
contemporary American mythologist, educator, writer
in *The Rebirth of the Hero*

What constitutes "personal authority"? Stated most simply, it means to find what is true for oneself and to live it in the world. If it is not lived, it is not real for us, and we abide in what Sartre called "bad faith," the theologian calls "sin," the therapist calls "neurosis," and the **existential** philosopher calls "inauthentic being." Respectful of the rights and perspectives of others, personal authority is neither narcissistic nor imperialistic. It is a humble acknowledgment of what wishes to come to being through us.

~ James Hollis Ph.D. (1940-present)
American Jungian analyst and author
in *Finding Meaning in the Second Half of Life*

Each man had only one genuine vocation--to find the way to himself ... His task was to discover his own destiny--not an arbitrary one--and live it out wholly and resolutely within himself. Everything else was only a would-be existence, an attempt at evasion, a flight back to the ideals of the masses, conformity and fear of one's own inwardness. The new vision rose up before me, glimpsed a hundred times, possibly even expressed before but now experienced for the first time by me. I was an experiment on the part of Nature, a gamble within the unknown, perhaps for a new purpose, perhaps for nothing, and my only task was to allow this game on the part of primeval depths to take its course, to feel its will within me and make it wholly mine.

~ The character of Demian, in *Demian*
by Herman Hesse (1877-1962)
German author

I must be myself. I cannot break myself any longer for you, or you. If you can love me for what I am, we shall be the happier. If you cannot, I will still seek to deserve that you should. I will not hide my tastes or aversions. I will so trust that what is deep is holy, that I will do strongly before the sun and moon whatever inly rejoices me, and the heart appoints.

~ Ralph Waldo Emerson (1803-1882)
American transcendentalist author, poet, and philosopher
"Self Reliance" in *Essays: First Series*

13

I think it's better to have my lyre or a chorus that I might lead out of tune and dissonant, and have the vast majority of men disagree with me and contradict me, than to be out of harmony with myself, to contradict myself, though I'm only one person.

~ Socrates (469-399 B.C.)
Greek philosopher
as reported by Plato in the dialogue *Gorgias*

This above all: to thine own self be true,
And it must follow, as the night the day,
Thou canst not then be false to any man.

~ The character of Polonious in *Hamlet*
by William Shakespeare (1564-1616)
English playwright

If other people do not understand our behavior--so what? Their request that we must only do what they understand is an attempt to dictate to us. If this is being "asocial" or "irrational" in their eyes, so be it. Mostly they resent our freedom and our courage to be ourselves. We owe nobody an explanation or an accounting, as long as our acts do not hurt or infringe on them.

~ Erich Fromm (1900-1980)
German psychoanalyst and humanistic philosopher
in *The Art of Being*

Our relationship to past symbols of authority is changing because we are awakening to ourselves as individual beings with an inner rulership.

~ M. C. Richards (1916-1999)
American author, poet, potter
in *The Crossing Point*

I shall be telling this with a sigh
Somewhere ages and ages hence:
Two roads diverged in a wood, and I –
I took the one less traveled by,
And that has made all the difference

~ Robert Frost (1874-1963)
American poet
in *The Road Less Travelled*

It is only when one has taken the leap into the unknown of total selfhood, psychological independence and unique individuality that one is free to proceed along still higher paths of spiritual growth and free to manifest love in its greatest dimensions.

~ M. Scott Peck (1936-2005)
American psychiatrist and author
in *The Road Less Traveled*

3

UNIQUENESS AND INDIVIDUALITY

We are not here to fit in, be well balanced, or provide exempla for others. We are here to be eccentric, different, perhaps strange, perhaps merely to add our small piece, our little clunky, chunky selves, to the great mosaic of being. As the gods intended, we are here to become more and more ourselves.

~ James Hollis Ph.D. (1940-present)
American Jungian analyst and author
in *What Matters Most*

Whether peering through the lens of quantum physics or ancient mysticism, the conclusion remains the same: all that exists is one. Nevertheless, whether from the sea of quantum particles or from the Absolute, waves of difference emerge and manifest as the cosmos, as you, as I.

Although we are not separate, we are different from each other. Each person is unique. Yes, our fingerprints leave unique traces. Yes, our DNA identifies only one person. Yes, the combinations of strengths, weaknesses, virtues, vices, and foibles differ. Perhaps most significant is that expression of being that you are who alone now peers out from your unrepeatable inwardness.

If you grant that you are unique, is that the end to learning how to be your own person? No. The question then becomes, how will you realize the potential of your unique difference? Will you bury it beneath conformity? Or will you accept and nurture your difference thereby becoming not merely a person, but an individual.

Psychology speaks of the path of acceptance and nurturing your difference as "individuation." As you individuate, you increasingly honor and reveal your uniqueness. Finally you come to rest at ease in the givenness of your very own unique nature.

◊ ◊ ◊

Uniqueness

A human being is a single being. Unique and unrepeatable.

~ Pope John Paul II (1920-2005)
Polish Roman Catholic pope, cardinal and priest

But every man is more than just himself; he also represents the unique, the very special and always significant and remarkable point at which the world's phenomena intersect only once in this way and never again.

~ The character of Demian, in *Demian*
by Herman Hesse (1877-1962)
German author

In his heart every man knows quite well that, being unique, he will be in the world only once and that no imaginable chance will for a second time gather together into a unity so strangely variegated an assortment such as he is....

~ Friedrich Nietzsche (1844-1900)
German philosopher
"Schopenhauer as Educator" in *The Untimely Meditations*

Positive freedom as the realization of the self implies the full affirmation of the uniqueness of the individual. Men are born equal but they are also born different. The basis of this difference is the inherited equipment, physiological and mental, with which they start life, to which is added the particular constellation of circumstances that they meet with.

~ Erich Fromm (1900-1980)
German psychoanalyst and humanistic philosopher
in *Escape from Freedom*

To love oneself is to struggle to rediscover and maintain your uniqueness. It is understanding and appreciating the idea that you will be the only you to ever live upon this earth, that when you die so will all of your fantastic possibilities. It is the realization that even you are not totally aware of the wonders which lie dormant within yourself.

~ Leo Buscaglia (1924-1998)
motivational speaker, author, professor
in *Love: What Life is All About*

While everyone and everything is an expression of the same Source, each is a unique expression of that Source. No wave is exactly like any other wave; no cloud is exactly like any other cloud. When you understand uniqueness from this perspective, you realize that uniqueness is not specialness, nor is it based on separateness.

~ A. H. Almaas (1944-present)
Kuwaiti-born American psychologist and philosopher
in *Facets of Unity*

What struck me when I read that in the thirteenth-century Queste de Saint Graal, was that it epitomizes an especially Western spiritual aim and ideal, which is, of living the life that is potential in you and was never in anyone else as a possibility.

This, I believe, is the great Western truth: that each of us is a completely unique creature and that, if we are ever to give any gift to the world, it will have to come out of our own experience and fulfillment of our own potentialities, not someone else's.

~ Joseph Campbell (1904-1987)
American educator and mythologist
in *The Power of Myth*

Individuality

Every person born into this world represents something new, something that never existed before, something original and unique. It is the duty of every person ... to know and consider ... that there has never been anyone like him in the world, for if there had been someone like him, there would have been no need for him to be in the world. Every single person is a new thing in the world and is called upon to fulfill his particularity in this world. Every person's foremost task is the actualization of his unique, unprecedented and never recurring potentialities, and not the repetition of something that another, be it even the greatest, has already achieved.

~ Martin Buber (1878-1965)
Jewish philosopher
in *The Way of Man: According to the Teaching of* **Hasidism**

On the quest for the Holy Grail, Campbell observed, each knight embarked on his own path into the dark forest, to embark on his own adventure, believing that it would be a disgrace to follow the path of another. The Holy Grail, a symbol for the culmination of spiritual realization, can only be attained, Campbell stressed, by the person who has lived his or her own life, not one who has followed the path of another. To attain the Grail, that is, you must become who you are, realize your unique potentiality, become a type unto yourself. For no one else exactly like you has ever lived before, no one exactly like you will ever live in the future.

~ Keiron Le Grice
contemporary American mythologist, educator, writer
in *The Rebirth of the Hero*

In becoming fully human, we are called to be individuals. We are called to be unique and different.

~ M. Scott Peck (1936-2005)
American psychiatrist and author
in *The Different Drum: Community Making and Peace*

Personality is the supreme realization of the innate idiosyncrasy of a living being. It is an act of high courage flung in the face of life ... True personality is always a vocation and puts its trust in it as in God, despite its being, as the ordinary man would say, only a personal feeling. But vocation acts like a law of God from which there is no escape. The fact that many a man who goes his own way ends in ruin means nothing to one who has a vocation. He must obey his own law. Anyone with a vocation hears the voice of the inner man: he is called.

~ Carl Jung (1875-1961)
Swiss depth psychologist
in *The Development of Personality, CW17*

If a man does not keep pace with his companions, perhaps it is because he hears a different drummer. Let him step to the music which he hears, however measured or far away. It is not important that he should mature as soon as an apple tree or an oak. Shall he turn his spring into summer?

~ Henry David Thoreau (1817-1862)
American transcendentalist, naturalist and author
in *Walden*

We are designed, coded, it seems, to place the highest priority on being individuals, and we must do this first, at whatever cost, even if it means disability for the group.

~ Lewis Thomas (1913-1993)
American physician, poet and etymologist
in *The Medusa and the Snail*

The eighteenth-century German philosopher Johann Herder taught that each person has an original and unique manner of being human. The task is to develop it. According to Nietzsche, a person is known by his "style," that is, by the unique pattern that gives unity and distinctiveness to a person's activities. Style articulates the uniqueness of the self. Rather than fitting one's life into the demands of external conformity, rather than living one's life as an imitation of the life of another, one should look to find the authentic self within. One should labor to develop one's own unique style in crafting one's soul. An individual who denies her own individuality articulates life with a voice other than that which is uniquely her own. A person who suppresses his own self is in danger of missing the point of his own existence, of surrendering what being human means.

~ Rabbi Byron L. Sherwin
contemporary American Jewish theologian
in *Crafting the Soul*

The wise Rabbi Bunam once said in old age, when he had already grown blind: "I should not like to change places with our father Abraham! What good would it do God if Abraham became like blind Bunam, and blind Bunam became like Abraham? Rather than have this happen, I think I shall try to become a little more myself."

~ Martin Buber (1878-1965)
Jewish philosopher
in *The Way of Man: According to the Teaching of Hasidism*

Once, the Hassidic rabbi Zusya came to his followers with tears in his eyes. They asked him: "Zusya what's the matter?"

And he told them about his vision; "I learned the question that the angels will one day ask me about my life."

The followers were puzzled. "Zusya, you are pious. You are scholarly and humble. You have helped so many of us. What question about your life could be so terrifying that you would be frightened to answer it?"

Zusya replied;"I have learned that the angels will not ask me, 'Why weren't you a Moses, leading your people out of slavery?' and that the angels will not ask me, 'Why weren't you a Joshua, leading your people into the promised land?'"

Zusya sighed;"They will say to me, 'Zusya, why weren't you Zusya?'"

~ Martin Buber (1878-1965)
Jewish philosopher
in *Tales of the Hasidim: The Early Masters*

The duty to be alive is the same as the duty to become oneself, to develop into the individual one potentially is.

~ Erich Fromm (1900-1980)
German psychoanalyst and humanistic philosopher
in *Man for Himself*

Remember always that you have not only the right to be an individual; you have an obligation to be one. You cannot make any useful contribution in life unless you do this.

~ Eleanor Roosevelt (1884-1962)
former first lady of the United States and humanitarian

There is only one you in the world, just one, and if that is not fulfilled, then something has been lost.

~ Martha Graham (1894-1991)
American choreographer

Become him who you are!

~ Pindar (522 BC–443 BC)
Greek Poet
cited in *Nietzsche: The Man and His* Philosophy by Reginald Hollingdale

If God had wanted me otherwise, He would have created me otherwise.

~ Johann Wolfgang von Goethe (1749-1832)
German poet, dramatist, novelist, and scientist

To be nobody-but-yourself
in a world which is doing its best,
night and day
to make you everybody else
means to fight the hardest battle
which any human being can fight;
and never stop fighting

~ e. e. cummings (1894-1962)
American poet
in *E. E. Cummings: Complete Poems, 1904-1962*

If a person possesses any tolerable amount of common sense and experience, his own mode of laying out his existence is best, not because it is best in itself, but because it is his own mode.

~ John Stuart Mill (1806-1873)
English philosopher and economist
in *Three Essays on Religion*

As many men, so many minds; every one his own way.

~ Terence (c. 195/185–c. 159 BC)
Roman playwright
"Phormio" in *Three of the Comedies of Terence: Andria, Adelphi and Phormio* translated by Henry Thomas Riley

To be one's self, and unafraid whether right or wrong, is more admirable than the easy cowardice of surrender to conformity.

~ Irving Wallace (1916-1990)
American author and screenwriter
in *The Square Pegs*

For what is a man? What has he got?
If not himself, then he has naught.
To say the things he truly feels,
And not the words of one who kneels;
The record shows I took the blows
And did it my way!

~ Revaux, Francois, and Anka
American songwriters
in the song, *My Way*

Individuation is the forging of a transparent vessel - the authentic person who brings through what is beyond the person in a uniquely personal way.

~ John Wellwood (1943-present)
American psychotherapist and author
"Double Vision" in *The Sacred Mirror* edited by John Prendergast

A person is authentic in that degree to which his being in the world is unqualifiedly in accord with the givenness of his own nature and of the world.

~ James Bugental (1915-2008)
American existential/humanistic psychotherapist and author
in *The Search for Authenticity*

4

PERSONAL AUTONOMY

One has to be a light to oneself; this light is the law. There is no other law.

~ Jiddu Krishnamurti (1895-1996)
Indian spiritual teacher and philosopher
in *Krishnamurti's Journal*

When persons consider autonomy, they often think of it in terms of independence from others' control of one's decisions and life course. Or they think of being self-governing, free from the meddling of others. However for as long as person conceive autonomy as being in opposition to another, the extraordinary freedom of autonomy will elude them.

If you are autonomous, you don't need to rebel from the control of another. The rebel's need to fight a person or institution implies his own enmeshment with the controller. His actions are a triggered response to the other, rather than sourced from within.

Similarly you don't need to exert independence from the presumed authority of others. Why arouse yourself needlessly when the only authority you acknowledge is that of your very own Self?

Going through life, bouncing like a billiard ball off of this and that event and person may seem like freedom, but the freedom to be reactive is neither free nor autonomous. We've all met persons who were imprisoned by their reactivity.

Instead when autonomous, you make your path through life with your attention resting inwardly, listening to discern and to discriminate the inarticulate thoughts (the tones, the felt sense) of your Heart (not your emotions) and intuition. What you hear guides you like a light on your path, and you act accordingly.

To some persons, your actions will be valued as self-directed or self-governing. Others may appreciate your actions as expressing personal authority. Certainly your actions will demonstrate your internalizing of your **locus of control**.

Yet for you, what others call autonomy is simplicity itself: the inherent freedom of living in accord with the Law of your Being.

The deepest problems of modern life derive from the claim of the individual to preserve the autonomy and individuality of his existence in the face of overwhelming social forces, of historical heritage, of external culture, and of the technique of life. The fight with nature which primitive man has to wage for his *bodily* existence attains in this modern form its latest transformation.

~ Georg Simmel (1858-1918)
German sociologist, philosopher, and critic
in *Sociology: Modern Readings*, edited by Anthony Giddens

'Autonomy' is in fact a more apt term than 'moral freedom' for capturing this conception of freedom: 'autonomy' means to make one's own laws and to administer them, to be self-legislating. An autonomous being is one which ordains for itself the principles by which it shall live, and is therefore self-governing.

~ Brian Fay
contemporary American philosopher
in *Critical Social Science*

Autonomy pertains to self-regulation: control and direction from within, rather than from any external authority.

Autonomy is expressed through an individual's capacity for independent survival (supporting and maintaining one's existence through productive work), independent thinking (looking at the world through one's own eyes), and independent judgment (honoring inner signals and values).

Autonomy should not be interpreted as self-sufficiency in the absolute sense. It does not mean that one lives on a desert island or should act as if one did.

~ Nathaniel Branden (1930-present)
American psychologist
in *Taking Responsibility*

The Philosophy of that law in Nature, which implants in man as well as in every beast a passionate, inherent, and instinctive desire for freedom and self-guidance, pertains to psychology and cannot be touched on now... Perhaps the best synthesis of this feeling is found in three lines in Milton's Paradise Lost. Says the "Fallen One": -

> "Here we may reign secure; and in my choice,
> To reign is worth ambition, though in Hell!
> Better to reign in Hell than serve in Heaven ..."

Better be man, the crown of terrestrial production and king over its *opus operatum*, than be lost among the will-less spiritual Host in Heaven.

~ H. P. Blavatsky (1831-1891)
Russian mystic and co-founder of the Theosophical Society
in *The Secret Doctrine*

Better Hell in one's own character than Heaven as somebody else, for that would be exactly to make Hell, Heaven, and of Heaven, Hell.

~ Joseph Campbell (1904-1987)
American educator and mythologist
in *Creative Mythology*

The highest manifestation of life consists in this: that a being governs its own actions. A thing which is subject to the direction of another is somewhat of a dead thing.

~ Thomas Aquinas (1225-1274)
influential Catholic philosopher and theologian
cited in *Modern Christian Revolutionaries* by Donald Attwater

It matters not how strait the gate,
How charged with punishments the scroll,
I am the master of my fate:
I am the captain of my soul.

~ William Henley (1849-1903)
English poet, critic, author
in *Invictus*

Sovereignty isn't something someone gives you ... It's a responsibility you carry inside yourself ... each man and woman among us has to be sovereign. Sovereignty begins with yourself.

~ Eddie Benton-Banai (1934-present)
Ojibwe spiritual elder
in *Wisdomkeepers* by Harvey Arden & Steve Wall

You are the master of your fate. But you must exercise this mastership.

~ Ernest Holmes (1887-1960)
American **Science of Mind** founder

It is by his freedom that a man knows himself, by his sovereignty over his own life that a man measures himself.

~ Elie Wiesel (1928-present)
Jewish American activist and author
in *From the Kingdom of Memory*

Over himself, over his own body and mind, the individual is sovereign.

~ John Stuart Mill (1806-1873)
English philosopher and economist
in *On Liberty*

Alone, you are a sovereign.
Yourself, a precious kingdom.
Reign with peace and harmony!
What external force can possibly invade?

~ Hanshan Deqing (1546-1623)
Chinese monk and teacher of **Chan** and **Pure Land Buddhism**

You will fetter my leg, but not Zeus himself can get the better of my free will.

~ Epictetus (c. 55–135)
Greek **Stoic** philosopher
in *The Works of Epictetus* translated by Thomas W. Higginson

Man can will nothing unless he has first understood that he must count on no one but himself; that he is alone, abandoned on earth in the midst of his infinite responsibilities, without help, with no other aim than the one he sets himself, with no other destiny than the one he forges for himself on this earth.

~ Jean-Paul Sartre (1905-1980)
French existential philosopher and author

In an attempt to gain or hold love, approval, esteem, the individual relinquishes the locus of evaluation which was his in infancy, and places it in others. He learns to have a basic distrust for his own experiencing as a guide to his behavior. He learns from others a large number of conceived values, and adopts them as his own, even though they may be widely discrepant from what he is experiencing. Because these concepts are not based on his own valuing, they tend to be fixed and rigid, rather than fluid and changing.

~ Carl Rogers (1902-1987)
American psychologist
in *The Carl Rogers Reader*

Another trend which is evident in this process of becoming a person relates to the source or locus of choices and decisions, or evaluative judgments. The individual increasingly comes to feel that his locus of evaluation lies within himself. Less and less does he look to others for approval or disapproval; for standards to live by; for decisions and choices. He recognizes that it rests within himself to choose; that the only question which matters is, "Am I living in a way which is deeply satisfying to me, and which truly expresses me?" This I think is perhaps the most important question for the creative individual.

~ Carl Rogers (1902-1987
American psychologist
in *On Becoming a Person*

Stepping into largeness will require that we discern our personal authority - rather than the authority of others or the authority of our internalized admonitions - and live this inner authority with risk and boldness.
~ James Hollis Ph.D. (1940-present)
American Jungian analyst and author
in *What Matters Most*

One has to be a light to oneself; this light is the law. There is no other law. All the other laws are made by thought and so fragmentary and contradictory. To be a light to oneself is not to follow the light of another, however reasonable, logical, historical, and however convincing. You cannot be a light to yourself if you are in the dark shadows of authority, of dogma, of conclusion.

~ Jiddu Krishnamurti (1895-1996)
Indian spiritual teacher and philosopher
in *Krishnamurti's Journal*

Staying within ourselves means staying within our own understanding, what we have actually realized, regardless of how deep or shallow that may be.

~ Rodney Smith (1947-present)
American Buddhist teacher
in *Awakening*

As soon as you trust yourself, you will know how to live.

~ Johann Wolfgang von Goethe (1749-1832
German poet, dramatist, novelist, and scientist

Drink from your own wells. Sup at your table. Speak from your own heart. Go where your legs take you. Know your own mind. See through your soul's eyes. Follow none but your own self. For each man has his own pathway, and whoever would be your guide cannot help but lead you astray.

~ Marcus Tullius Tiro (c.103 BC-4 BC)
Roman author
cited in *Humanistic Psychology* by C. William Tageson

I am not a Federalist, because I never submitted the whole system of my opinions to the creed of any party of men whatever in religion, in philosophy, in politics, or in anything else where I was capable of thinking for myself. Such an addiction is the last degradation of a free and moral agent. If I could not go to heaven but with a party, I would not go there at all.

~ Thomas Jefferson (1743-1845)
American president
in a *Letter to Francis Hopkinson, March 13, 1789*

A saner man would have found himself, often enough "in formal opposition" to what are deemed "the most sacred laws of society," through obedience to yet more sacred laws, and so have tested his resolution without going out of his way. It is not for a man to put himself in such an attitude to society, but to maintain himself in whatever attitude he find himself through obedience to the laws of his being, which will never be one of opposition to a just government, if he should chance to meet with such.

~ Henry David Thoreau (1817-1862)
American transcendentalist, naturalist, and author
in *Walden*

It is easy in the world to live after the world's opinion. It is easy in solitude to live our own. But the great man is he who in the midst of the crowd keeps with perfect sweetness the independence of solitude.

~ Ralph Waldo Emerson (1803-1882)
American transcendentalist author, poet, and philosopher
"Self Reliance" in *Essays: First Series*

Be yourself and think for yourself; and while your conclusions may not be infallible, they will be nearer right than the conclusions forced upon you.

~ Elbert Hubbard (1856-1915)
American philosopher and writer

I studiously avoided all so-called "holy men." I did so because I had to make do with my own truth, not accept from others what I could not attain on my own. I would have felt it as a theft had I attempted to learn from the holy men and to accept their truth for myself. Neither in Europe can I make any borrowings from the East, but must shape my life out of myself--out of what my inner being tells me, or what nature brings to me.

~ Carl Jung (1875-1961)
Swiss depth psychologist
in *Memories, Dreams, Reflections*

5

THE QUESTION OF MORALITY

One who surpasses his fellow citizens in virtue is no longer a part of the city. Their law is not for him, since he is a law to himself.

~ Aristotle (384 BC-322 BC)
Greek philosopher
cited in *Thoreau 1862* by Ralph Waldo Emerson

As you exercise your personal autonomy, you may occasionally find yourself in conflict with society's moral standards. At such times, distinguishing between moral standards and the benevolence which sometimes inspires them may help you to discern your path forward.

Moral standards are not absolute. They can vary from culture to culture. For example, where a Muslim might dutifully execute an infidel for religious reasons, also for religious reasons a Buddhist might beg for mercy for that infidel.

Furthermore, a moral standard is a construct of thought which would guide you, but at a debilitating cost. Thought divides you into dualities such as good/evil, right/wrong, and spiritual/unspiritual. Half of you is praised, the other half despised.

But as we will see in later sections, psychologists who would guide you to become yourself and spiritual teachers who would guide you to become realized emphatically disagree with the tyranny of dualism.

Where thought slices and dices reality, the sun simply shares its light with what some teachers have called the "natural perfection" of all that is. Perhaps reality, what is, suggests a deeper code than condemning an artificial half of existence. Certainly psychological individuation requires living more deeply than seeing your actions as good and bad.

If you are autonomous, for you the issue of morality is not whether you are moral or amoral. Instead what concerns you is the *source* of the moral authority that guides you. Is it the crowd or the law of your own being?

Some persons will object to your following the law of your being as the higher moral authority. They fear it will lead to moral anarchy. Certainly persons could abuse this seeming freedom. But for individuals who are more intimate with the innate benevolence of their true nature, this need not be a concern.

Rightdoing and Wrongdoing?

Whether you are bound by a gold chain or an iron one, you are in captivity. Your virtuous activities are the gold chain, your evil ones the iron one. He who shakes off both the chains of good and evil that imprison him, him I call a Brahmin - he has attained the Supreme Truth.

~ Angelus Silesius (1624-1677)
German Catholic priest, mystic, and religious poet
in *The Book of Angelus Silesius* by Frederick Franck

The free man is immoral because he is determined in everything to depend upon himself and not upon some tradition.

~ Friedrich Nietzsche (1844-1900)
German philosopher
cited in *Nietzsche: The Man and His Philosophy* by R. J. Hollingdale

Our behavior and expressions are controlled by a superego, with its lists of Do's and Don'ts and the power to punish if one violates its commandments. The superego is the internalization of the "dictatorial" parent…. Dethroning the superego and restoring and individual's freedom of expression does not turn him into an uncivilized being; rather, it is a condition that allows him to be a responsible member of society, a truly moral person. Only a free person is respectful of the rights and freedom of others.

~ Alexander Lowen M.D. (1910-2008)
American founder of **Bioenergetic** Therapy
in *Joy*

Oh you can walk the straight and narrow,
But with a little bit o' luck,
you'll run amuck!
They're always throwin' goodness at you,
But with a little bit o' luck,
A man can duck!

~ "With a Little Bit of Luck" song from *My Fair Lady* (1964)
by Alan Lerner (1918-1986) and Fredrick Loewe (1904-1988)
American songwriters

I remember an answer which when quite young I was prompted to make to a valued adviser who was wont to importune me with the dear old doctrines of the church. On my saying, "What have I to do with the sacredness of traditions, if I live wholly from within?" my friend suggested – "But these impulses may be from below, not from above." I replied, "They do not seem to me to be such; but if I am the Devil's child, I will live then from the Devil." No law can be sacred to me but that of my nature. Good and bad are but names very readily transferable to that or this; the only right is what is after my constitution; the only wrong what is against it.

~ Ralph Waldo Emerson (1803-1882)
American transcendentalist author, poet, and philosopher,
"Self Reliance" in *Essays: First Series*

The actual experience of ... taking possession of one's own standards of morality is usually one of joyful liberation. For the first time one is really free to choose; and a person who has worked at the level of the Fellowcraft and has come to terms with the compelling and constraining material in his unconscious can lay claim to genuine free will.

But there is a genuine risk here too; free will is a truly dangerous thing. If the process of psychological growth is seen only as the discarding of compulsion and conventional standards of right and wrong and the replacing of them with one's personal standards of morality, the person working at the level of the Fellowcraft becomes an entirely free agent, responsible to no one but himself. Because such a situation can lead easily to self-indulgent and opportunistic behavior it is at this point that **Freemasonry** and the schools of psychology based on the scientific paradigm of the twentieth century diverge sharply. From the viewpoint of Freemasonry there is much more to this process than simply the acquisition of free will - important as that is.

~ W. Kirk MacNulty
contemporary British Freemason
in *Freemasonry*

This understanding of nonconceptual positivity is a very unusual idea, since ordinarily, and at the beginning of working on oneself, we think that there are things that are good and things that are bad. As we progress, we realize that this discrimination is only subjective, that dividing things into good and bad is arbitrary.

~ A. H. Almaas (1944-present)
Kuwaiti-born American psychologist and philosopher
in *Facets of Unity*

There is nothing either good or bad but thinking makes it so.

~ The character of Hamlet in *Hamlet*
by William Shakespeare (1564-1616)
English playwright

There are no moral phenomena, only a moral interpretation of phenomena.

~ Friedrich Nietzsche (1844-1900)
German philosopher
in *Beyond Good & Evil: Prelude to a Philosophy of the Future*

Questioner: What is right and what is wrong varies with habit and custom. Standards vary with societies.

Nisargadatta Maharaj: Discard all traditional standards. Leave them to the hypocrites. Only what liberates you from desire and fear and wrong ideas is good. As long as you worry about sin and virtue you will have no peace.

Q: I grant that sin and virtue are social norms. But there may be also spiritual sins and virtues. I mean by spiritual the absolute. Is there such a thing as absolute sin or absolute virtue?

N: Sin and virtue refer to a person only. Without a sinful or virtuous person what is sin or virtue? At the level of the absolute there are no persons; the ocean of pure awareness is neither virtuous nor sinful. Sin and virtue are invariably relative.

~ Nisargadatta Maharaj (1897-1981)
Indian guru of Shiva **Advaita nondualism**
in *I am That*

In spiritual work, concepts of a devil, of dark forces, of some evil that exists on its own outside of the goodness of reality are considered manifestation of ignorance, both in terms of believing in such concepts and in terms of the manifestations attributed to such forces. All spiritual work would be pointless if there were such a thing as ultimate evil.

~ A. H. Almaas (1944-present)
Kuwaiti-born American psychologist and philosopher
in *Facets of Unity*

The wise understand all of life amid the ten thousand things as basically a play of forces. Moral teachings that attempt to break the complementary relation of "good" and "evil" are doomed to failure, and breed violence to others and to oneself. This teaching is an essential aspect of the doctrine that has, in the Western world, often been condemned as heretical or dangerous. In any case it is always a difficult, hidden, and subtle doctrine, easily misunderstood as justifying self-indulgence and even cruelty. Nietzsche's famous "beyond good and evil" echoes this doctrine, and the crimes that have been committed under this banner are ample testimony to the need to understand it only in the context of a complete spiritual teaching. In Judaism and Islam this idea often forms part of the "esoteric" path, reserved for those who have passed through the moral discipline and training of the "exoteric" or orthodox tradition. Every complete religious tradition comprises these different levels of understanding and practice.

~ Gia Fu Feng (1919-1985)
Chinese teacher of **Taoism**
in *Tao Te Ching* by Lao Tze and Gia Fu Feng

Natural Perfection

All Nature is but Art unknown to thee;
All chance, direction which thou canst not see;
All discord, harmony not understood;
All partial evil, universal good;
And spite of Pride, in erring Reason's spite,
One truth is clear: Whatever is, is right.

~ Alexander Pope (1688-1744)
English poet and writer
in *Essay on Man*

Tao is the source of the ten thousand things.

~ Lao Tsu (c.604 BC–c.521 BC)
Taoist philosopher
in the *Tao Te Ching*

For everything that lives is holy, life delights in life.

~ William Blake (1757-1827)
British poet
in *America: A Prophecy*

Ema! Phenomena are, without exception,
Perfect within the continuum of self-arising **rigpa**.

~ cited by H. H. Dalai Lama (1935–present)
in *Dzogchen: The Heart Essence of the Great Perfection*

Now is the time for the world to know
That every thought and action is sacred.
This is the time
For you to deeply compute the impossibility
That there is anything
But Grace.
Now is the season to know
That everything you do
Is sacred.

~ Hafiz (c. 1310-1406)
Persian poet and Sufi master
"Now is the Time" in *The Gift* translated by Daniel Ladinsky

Some might misunderstand and wonder: Then why bother with virtuous actions and accumulating merits or helping others? Why generate loving-kindness and compassion? Others might think: Why not continue to perform negative actions, since in emptiness everything is equal? This is a grave misunderstanding. This is a danger, a deviation from the view. This is nihilism, where the yawning abyss of pseudo-emptiness beckons.

~ Nyoshul Khenpo (1932-2001)
Tibetan Buddhist Dzogchen master
in *Natural Great Perfection*

This does not mean that you have the license to do whatever you want, justifying it with "all action is perfect." Only one who is established in Holy Perfection, who continuously perceives it, can act totally spontaneously. This action will naturally be an expression of fundamental goodness and love.

~ A. H. Almaas (1944-present)
Kuwaiti-born American psychologist and philosopher
in *Facets of Unity*

There are two aspects here, the view and the conduct. You need to distinguish between them. These are two different aspects which you cannot – and should not – simply fuse into one....

In terms of the view, there is nothing to accept or reject. However, if one doesn't accept what is good and reject evil – if one doesn't accept the **Dharma** or reject mundane aims – one simply goes on living a worldly life. In short, you need to distinguish between view and conduct...

To lose the conduct in the view means that the view, which is emptiness is superimposed upon all one's actions...Then one becomes uncaring and frivolous and doesn't discriminate between help and harm, good and evil. That is called losing the conduct in the view. Please be careful to avoid this mistake!

The other extreme is lose the view in the conduct, to only think in terms of good and evil, what is virtuous and unvirtuous. **Guru Rinpoche** also said, "If you lose the view in conduct, you will never have the chance to be liberated." It is through the view that one is liberated. If you lose the view in the conduct, you will never have the opportunity to be free. If you lose the conduct in the view, then you ignore the difference between good and evil.

~ Tulku Urgyen Rinpoche (1920-1995)
Tibetan Buddhist Dzogchen Master
in *As It Is, Vol. II*

Out beyond ideas of wrongdoing and rightdoing, there is a field. I'll meet you there.

~ Jalal ad-Din Muhammad Rumi (1207-1273)
Persian poet and Sufi master
"A Great Wagon" in *The Essential Rumi* translated by Coleman Barks

6

PSYCHOLOGICAL WHOLENESS

For the good man to realize that it is better to be whole than to be good is to enter on a straight and narrow path compared to which his previous rectitude was flowery license.

~ John Middleton Murry (1889-1957)
English literary critic

Moral standards not only divide behavior into good and bad dualities, but also they divide us into good and bad parts. To become ourselves, we need to reclaim all that we are, for much of who we are has been banished to our unconscious.

During childhood, socialization transforms us from little animals to participating members of society. "Do this!" "Don't do that!" "Good girl!" "Bad boy!" Slowly we learn what our parents and society favor, what they reject.

Gradually we take on the values of our childhood authorities. We internalize what they favor, and we reject what they reject. What we were praised for, we like and identify with. What we were criticized, rejected, or punished for, we dislike, reject, and exile from our awareness. The inner critic becomes alive to rule with a clenched-fist tyranny.

But those unwanted parts don't go away. They sleep in the unconscious. Occasionally they erupt into waking consciousness causing embarrassment. Sometimes they unsettle us with disturbing dreams. Many persons refer to those unwanted parts as "the shadow".

Like it or not, the shadow is part of who you are. And if you are to truly become yourself, then your shadow will need to become integrated into your waking life. Individuation requires this of us. For how can you become who you are, if you do not become *all* that you are?

For the person who walks the path of personal authenticity, the aspiration that guides him is not to become good, not to shun evil, but to become psychologically whole.

Living by principles is not living your own life. It is easier to try to be better than you are than to be who you are.

~ Marion Woodman (1928-present)
Canadian author and Jungian analyst
in *Addicted to Perfection*

He who follows the middle way knows an all-embracingness that excludes or changes nothing. This is not an easy way, for it requires a refinement of consciousness.

~ Helena Roerich (1879-1955)
Russian mystic and author
in *Supermundane: The Inner Life, Book Two*

Be ye whole, even as your Father in Heaven is whole.

~ Jesus of Nazareth (7–2 BC to 30–33 AD)
Matthew 5:48
Holy Bible, New Revised Standard Version

It seems that it is the purpose of evolution now to replace an image of perfection with the concept of completeness or wholeness. Perfection suggests something all pure, with no blemishes, dark spots or questionable areas. Wholeness includes the darkness but combines it with the light elements into a totality more real and whole than any ideal. This is an awesome task, and the question before us is whether mankind is capable of this effort and growth. Ready or not, we are in that process.

~ Robert A. Johnson (1921-present)
American Jungian analyst and author
in *He*

If you bring forth what is within you, what you bring forth will save you. If you do not bring forth what is within you, what you do not bring forth will destroy you.

~ Jesus of Nazareth (7–2 BC to 30–33 AD)
"Gospel of Thomas" in *Beyond Belief*
by Elaine Pagels

The spirit needs spring and winter, beauty and terror, meeting and parting, needs every experience and every energy to achieve wholeness. Milarepa said, "Contemplate all energies without fear or disgust; find their essence, for that is the stone that turns everything to gold."

~ Thuksey Rinpoche (1916-1983)
Tibetan Buddhist Master, in *A Journey in Ladakh*
by Andrew Harvey

I am a human being, nothing human is alien to me.

~ Terence (c. 195/185 – c. 159 BC)
Roman playwright

Real liberation comes not from glossing over or repressing painful states of feeling, but only from experiencing them to the full.

~ Carl Jung (1875-1961)
Swiss depth psychologist
in *The Archetypes and the Collective Unconscious*

When enlightenment happens, the organism does not become perfect. It is whole and the whole includes both opposites. Seeking perfections is the basic, primary folly and the **jnani** understands that.

~ Ramesh Balsekar (1917-2009)
Indian Advaita Vedanta teacher
in *Consciousness Speaks*

A whole person is one who has both walked with God and wrestled with the devil.

~ Carl Jung (1875-1961)
Swiss depth psychologist

Accepting the whole range of one's feelings, expressing them and gaining self-possession are the signposts along the road one travels on the voyage of self-discovery.

~ Alexander Lowen M.D. (1910-2008)
American founder of Bioenergetic Therapy
in *Joy*

Most people would prefer to get rid of their despair so that they only experience bliss. But this is a form of fascism – spiritual fascism – which wants only bliss. Bliss feels good and makes you happy, while despair feels bad, and you want it out of your sight. This tendency gives rise to the totalitarian point of view, whether material or spiritual.

~ Gangaji (1942-present)
American spiritual teacher
in *The Diamond in Your Pocket*

What is implied by the fulfillment of the new ethical demand is that the share of evil "allotted" to an individual by his constitution or personal fate should be worked through and deliberately endured by him. In the process, to an extent which varies with the individual, part of the negative side must be consciously lived. And it is no small part of the task of depth psychology to enable the individual to become capable of living in this world by acquiring the moral courage not to want to be either worse or better than he actually is.

~ Erich Neumann (1905-1960)
Jungian analyst and author
in *Depth Psychology and a New Ethic*

The great epochs of our life come when we gain the courage to rechristen our evil as what is best in us.

~ Friedrich Nietzsche (1844-1900)
German philosopher
in *Beyond Good & Evil*

"When you know something of **Abraxas** you cannot do this any longer. You aren't allowed to be afraid of anything, you can't consider prohibited anything that the soul desires."
Startled, I countered: "But you can't do everything that comes to mind! You can't kill someone because you detest him."
He moved closer to me.

"Under certain circumstances, even that. Yet it is a mistake most of the time. I don't mean that you should simply do everything that pops into your head. No. But you shouldn't harm and drive away those ideas that make good sense by exorcising them or moralizing about them. Instead of crucifying yourself or someone else you can drink wine from a chalice and contemplate the mystery of the sacrifice. Even without such procedures you can treat your drives and so-called temptations with respect and love. Then they will reveal their meaning--and they all do have meaning."

~ The character of Demian in *Demian*
by Herman Hesse (1877-1962)
German author

We have to look courageously in the face of the reality and see that it is God and none else who has made this world in His being and that so He has made it. We have to see that Nature devouring her children, Time eating up the lives of creatures, Death universal and ineluctable, and the violence of the **Rudra** forces in man and Nature are also the supreme Godhead in one of His cosmic figures. We have to see that God the bountiful and prodigal creator, God the helpful, strong, and benignant preserver is also God the devourer and destroyer. The torment of the couch of pain and evil on which we are racked is His touch as much as happiness and sweetness and pleasure. It is only when we see with the eye of the complete union and feel this truth in the depths of our being that we can entirely discover behind that mask, too, the calm and beautiful face of the all-blissful Godhead, and in this touch that tests our imperfection the touch of the friend and builder of the spirit in man. The discords of the world are God's discords, and it is only by accepting and proceeding through them that we can arrive at the greater concords of His supreme harmony...

~ Sri Aurobindo (1872-1950)
Indian philosopher, mystic, poet, and nationalist
cited by Satprem in *What is Enlightenment?* edited by J. White

It is right it should be so;
Man was made for Joy & Woe;
And when this we rightly know
Thro' the World we safely go.
Joy & Woe are woven fine,
A Clothing for the Soul divine;
Under every grief & pine
Runs a joy with silken twine.

~ William Blake (1757-1827)
British poet
in *Auguries of Innocence*

Revile not the world, for God - He is the world.

~ the Prophet Muhummad (570-632)

The persona ... contains in varying proportions, characteristics and tendencies which are currently considered in terms of good and bad, desirable and undesirable. In trying to improve himself consciously, the individual denies those tendencies which he considers undesirable, and rejects them. But such rejected tendencies do not really vanish; they remain and accumulate under the surface. Such suppression is the root cause of many mental disturbances. The realization of the fact that the unwanted aspects of one's ego are an integral part of what makes for a supposed individual is the first step towards relief through surrender.

Once there is a basic realization of - and acceptance of - the oneness of the good and the bad within the individual ego, all that is really needed is letting-go and witnessing of the operation of this realization.

~ Ramesh Balsekar (1917-2009)
Indian Advaita Vedanta teacher
in *The Final Truth*

Filling the conscious mind with ideal conceptions is a characteristic of Western theosophy, but not the confrontation with the shadow and the world of darkness. One does not become enlightened by imagining figures of light, but by making the darkness conscious.

~ Carl Jung (1875-1961)
Swiss depth psychologist
in *Alchemical Studies*

The perfection of wisdom alone can keep selflessness and love pure and steady under all conditions. Such is the realization of perfect wisdom through the entire body, speech, and mind of the **bodhisattva** who is free from controlling, battling, repressing, or extinguishing any form of manifestation.

~ Gautama Buddha (c. 563 BCE-483 BCE)
cited in *Mother of the Buddhas* by Lex Hixon

I would rather be whole than good.

~ Carl Jung (1875-1961)
Swiss depth psychologist

Individuation does not shut one out from the world, but gathers the world to oneself.

~ Carl Jung (1875-1961)
Swiss depth psychologist
in *The Structure and Dynamics of the Psyche*

Everything living dreams of individuation, for everything strives towards its own wholeness.

~ Carl Jung (1875-1961)
Swiss depth psychologist
in *The Wisdom of Carl Jung* edited by Edward Hoffman, Ph.D.

The road of excess leads to the palace of wisdom.

~ William Blake (1757-1827)
British poet
in *The Marriage of Heaven and Hell*

If the fool would persist in his folly he would become wise.

~ William Blake (1757-1827)
British poet
in *The Marriage of Heaven and Hell*

Better is one's own dharma though imperfect, than the dharma of another well performed. He who does the duty ordained by his own nature incurs no sin.

~ Krishna
supreme deity of Hinduism
in *Bhagavad Gita* translated by Swami Nikhilananda

To be on the safe side
I took out the fine-tooth
comb of retrospection to
run it through my life –

to comb out all
the dark dirty bits
of my history; the
silly messy naughty
mistakes

After combing furiously
for several hours I had
gotten rid of all the
nasty little lumps

I had now turned
myself into a piece
of HUMAN CONFECTIONERY;
what a success!
I had attained
MARSHAMALLOWDOM
the highest, most
attractive and
perfect state of
being and the
epitome of
GETTING IT RIGHT.

I was also stuck to the chair,
but more about
that later...

~ Michael Leunig (1945-present)
Australian cartoonist and poet
in *The Stick and Other Tales of Our Times*

Suppose you scrub your ethical skin until it shines, but inside there is no music, then what?

~ Kabir (1440-1518)
Indian mystic poet and saint
cited in *Transitions* by Julia Cameron

This being human is a guest house.
Every morning a new arrival.
A joy, a depression, a meanness,
some momentary awareness comes
as an unexpected visitor.

Welcome and entertain them all!
Even if they're a crowd of sorrows,
who violently sweep your house
empty of its furniture,
still, treat each guest honorably.
He may be clearing you out
for some new delight.

The dark thought, the shame, the malice,
meet them at the door laughing,
and invite them in.

Be grateful for whoever comes,
because each has been sent
as a guide from beyond.

~ Jalal ad-Din Muhammad Rumi (1207-1273)
Persian poet and Sufi master
"The Guest House" in *The Essential Rumi* translated by Coleman Barks

7

THE QUESTION OF BELIEFS

The sacred books of the East are nothing but words. I looked through their covers one day sideways. What Kabir talks of is only what he has lived through. If you have not lived through something, it is not true.

~ Kabir (1440-1518)
Indian mystic poet and saint

Beliefs are *reports* by others by which we choose to live, reports about the nature of the Mystery in which we live. But would you rather live a report about the Mystery or experience it? Would you rather be a believer or a knower? Would you be authentic were you to spend your life never questioning the beliefs your society taught you to believe?

For many persons, beliefs provide certainty. Believers don't just believe, they think they *know* the nature of existence. That certainty provides a raft of security on which they cling amid the frightening, turbulent waves of change in this sea of existential uncertainty we call life. However, strong swimmers don't entrust their lives to such fragile rafts. Instead they set off amid the waves for the rumored shores of personal knowledge.

Authenticity requires not only that we question beliefs with regard to their use for security, but also we question the capacity of a belief to represent truth. Scientists estimate the expanding universe contains one hundred billion galaxies, each of which contains several hundred billion stars. Existence, the universe, is seemingly infinite! Can its Mystery be captured in handfuls of words?

At best beliefs are pointers to truth, but not truth itself, just as the reflection of the moon is not the moon. What is truth? Spiritual teachers suggest it will not be found in words. Whatever it may be, find it, if you can, through your personal experience.

Certainty or Inquiry?

If you wish to strive for peace of soul and pleasure, then believe; if you wish to be a devotee of truth, then inquire.

~ Friedrich Nietzsche (1844-1900)
German philosopher

The quest for certainty blocks the search for meaning. Uncertainty is the very condition to impel man to unfold his powers.

~ Erich Fromm (1900-1980)
German psychoanalyst and social philosopher
in *Man for Himself*

The human understanding when it has once adopted an opinion (either as being the received opinion or as being agreeable to itself) draws all things else to support and agree with it. And though there be a greater number and weight of instances to be found on the other side, yet these it either neglects and despises, or else by some distinction sets aside and rejects, in order that by this great and pernicious predetermination the authority of its former conclusions may remain inviolate.

~ Francis Bacon (1561-1626)
English philosopher, scientists, author
in *Novum Organum*

If you would be a real seeker after truth, it is necessary that at least once in your life you doubt, as far as possible, all things.

~ Renee Descartes (1596-1650)
French philosopher

Mature psychological health cannot exist unless we are capable of doubting any form of conceptual certitude about ourselves or anything else.

~ Richard Moss MD
contemporary American spiritual teacher
in *The Mandala of Being*

We can be as honest as we are ignorant. If we are, when asked what is beyond the horizon of the known, we must say that we do not know.

~ Robert G. Ingersoll (1833-1899)
American orator known as "The Great Agnostic"

The man who has successfully solved the problem of his relations with the two worlds of data and symbols is a man who has no beliefs. With regard to the problems of practical life he entertains a series of working hypotheses, which serve his purposes, but are taken no more seriously than any other kind of tool or instrument.
In other words, symbols should never be raised to the rank of dogmas, nor should any system be regarded as more than a provisional convenience.

~ Aldous Huxley (1894-1963)
English writer
in *The Perennial Philosophy*

Freedom From Belief

What is important is to see that words and ideas enslave us in formulas and concepts. As long as we are trapped in a net of consoling belief, we lack the intensity and subtlety required for real exploration. Unless I understand this, my observation will remain based on forms, on what I know, and will not be enlivened by the spirit of discovery, as if for the first time. And it will be egocentric, with my ordinary "I" interpreting everything that is presented from its self-centered perspective.

~ Jeanne De Salzmann (1889-1990)
master teacher of the **Fourth Way** of **G. I. Gurdjieff**
in *The Reality of Being*

The issue here is the belief that you know. You believe that you know who you are, you believe that you know the world, you believe that you know what existence is. What you actually know is your own mind. You don't know existence. You have lost the mystery that you live in. We all lose the mystery that we are, the mystery that surrounds us, the mystery that brings us wonder, freshness, and freedom. We have made our world into a fossil.

~ A. H. Almaas (1944-present)
Kuwaiti-born American psychologist and philosopher
in *Diamond Heart Book Four: Indestructible Innocence*

If we are to reach certainty and true autonomy of realization, we need to be willing to be heretics. What's more, we need to become universal heretics, not believing anything that we do not know from direct experience, beyond stories, beyond hearsay, and even beyond the mind.

~ A. H. Almaas (1944-present)
Kuwaiti-born American psychologist and philosopher
in *Diamond Heart Five: Inexhaustible Mystery*

Until college and minaret have crumbled
This holy work of ours will not be done
Until faith becomes rejection
And rejection belief
There will be no True Believer.

~ Abu-Said Abul-Khayr (967–1049)
Persian poet and Sufi
cited in *The Way of The Sufi* by Idries Shah

None attains to the Degree of Truth until a thousand honest people have testified that he is a heretic.

~ Junayd of Baghdad (d. 910)
Sufi Master
cited in *The Way of The Sufi* by Idries Shah

Do not believe in anything simply because you have heard it. Do not believe in anything simply because it is spoken and rumored by many. Do not believe in anything simply because it is found written in your religious books. Do not believe in anything merely on the authority of your teachers and elders. Do not believe in traditions because they have been handed down for many generations. But after observation and analysis, when you find that anything agrees with reason and is conducive to the good and benefit of one and all, then accept it and live up to it.

~ Gautama Buddha (c. 563 BCE-483 BCE)

Ye say, ye believe in Zarathustra? But of what account is Zarathustra! Ye are my believers: but of what account are all believers!

Ye had not yet sought yourselves: then did ye find me. So do all believers; therefore all belief is of so little account.

Now do I bid you lose me and find yourselves ...

~ The character of Zarathustra in *Thus Spake Zarathustra*
by Friedrich Nietzsche (1844-1900)
German philosopher

"What of your training, Hercules, my son? ..."
"... One thing, O Teacher, I must tell to you and thus deceive you not. The fact is not so long ago I slew all those who taught me in the past. I killed my teachers, and in my search for liberty, I now stand free. I seek to know myself, within myself and through myself."
"My son, that was a deed of wisdom, and now you can stand free. Proceed to labour now ..."

~ The characters of Hercules and his Teacher in *The Labours of Hercules*
by Alice A. Bailey (1880-1949)
American **esotericist**

True states of realization occur when you throw away all the teachings. All of the teachings, absolutely. Everything. Then you are investigation itself finding out what you are.

~ A. H. Almaas (1944-present)
Kuwaiti-born American psychologist and philosopher
in *Inexhaustible Mystery: Diamond Heart Book Five*

Every thing possible to be believ'd is an image of truth.

~ William Blake (1757-1827)
British poet
in *The Marriage of Heaven and Hell*

◊ ◊ ◊

Beyond Words

I have a thousand brilliant lies
For the question:
What is God?
If you think that the Truth can be known
From words,
If you think that the Sun and the Ocean
Can pass through that tiny opening Called the mouth,
O someone should start laughing!
Someone should start wildly Laughing – Now!

~ Hafiz (c. 1310-1406)
Persian poet and Sufi master
"Someone Should Start Laughing" in *I Heard God Laughing* translated by Daniel Ladinsky

Whatever can be understood or perceived can never be the eternal Truth. The Unknown is the Truth.

~ Nisargadatta Maharaj (1897-1981)
Indian guru of Shiva Advaita nondualism
in *Prior to Consciousness*

The Tao that can be told is not the eternal Tao. The name that can be named is not the eternal name. The nameless is the beginning of heaven and earth.

~ Lao Tsu (c.604 BC–c.521 BC)
Taoist philosopher

Although all spiritual teachings originate from the same Source, once they become verbalized and written down they are obviously no more than a collection of words -- and a word is nothing more than a signpost.

~ Eckhart Tolle (1948-present)
German-born spiritual teacher
in *The Power of Now: A Guide to Spiritual Enlightenment*

The God that can be named is not God.

~ Soren Kierkegaard (1813–1855)
Danish philosopher, theologian, religious writer
cited in *What Matters Most* by James Hollis Ph.D.

'What is truth?' a disciple asked **Nasrudin**.
'Something which I have never, at any time, spoken - nor shall I.'

~ Idries Shah (1924-1996)
Indian Sufi author and teacher
in *The Pleasantries of the Incredible Mulla Nasrudin*

He who knows, knows not. He who knows not, knows.

~ Lao Tsu (c.604 BC–c.521 BC
Taoist philosopher
in the *Tao Te Ching*

Ah, more than any priest O soul we too believe in God. /But with the
mystery of God we dare not dally.

~ Walt Whitman (1819-1892)
American poet,
"Passage to India" in *The Complete Poems*

Furthermore, I shall explain the nature of **dharmata**:
Such a nature as this cannot be determined to be any one thing.
So however you label it, that is how it appears.

~ cited by H. H. Dalai Lama (1935–present)
from "The Reverberation of Sound" in *Dzogchen: The Heart Essence of
the Great Perfection*

I maintain that truth is a pathless land, and you cannot approach it by any path whatsoever, by any religion, by any sect. That is my point of view, and I adhere to that absolutely and unconditionally. Truth, being limitless, unconditioned, unapproachable by any path whatsoever cannot be organized; nor should any organization be formed to lead or to coerce people along any particular path. If you first understand that, then you will see how impossible it is to organize a belief. A belief is purely an individual matter, and you cannot and must not organize it. If you do, it becomes dead, crystallized; it becomes a creed, a sect, a religion, to be imposed on others.

~ Jiddu Krishnamurti (1895-1996)
Indian spiritual teacher and philosopher,
text from the 1929 speech, dissolving the Order of the Star
in *Krishnamurti: 100 Years by Evelyne Blau*

So as we sort through the rubble of historically charged images, by what standard do we gather them to our heart? It cannot be their institutional authority alone. It cannot be because our family or ethnic tradition embraced them. It can only be if they move us, that is set off a resonance within us. If such resonance occurs, the activation of like to like in some hidden harmony, then we know that that image has some meaning for us. We feel it.

~ James Hollis Ph.D. (1940-present)
American Jungian analyst and author
in *Finding Meaning in the Second Half of Life*

Believe those who are seeking truth, doubt those who find it, doubt all, but do not doubt yourself.

~ Andre Gide (1869-1951)
French critic, essayist, and novelist

8

PSYCHOLOGICAL AGENCY

We have made you a creature neither of heaven nor of earth, neither mortal nor immortal, in order that you may, as the free and proud shaper of your own being, fashion yourself in the form you may prefer. It will be in your power to descend to the lower, brutish forms of life; you will be able, through your own decision to rise again to the superior orders whose life is divine.

~ Giovanni Pico della Mirandola (1463-1494)
Italian humanist
in *Oration On the Dignity of Man*

Psychological agency is your capacity to act in and upon your world. With regard to being your own person, your agency actualizes your potential, and thereby you become truly yourself in an individual way. Choice, will, and action are the tools of your agency.

At birth, you are pure potential. Like a block of marble cut from the quarry of life, you could become any one of innumerable possibilities hidden within your block. With choice, you place the chisel. With will and action, your hammer strikes. Relinquished possibilities, the debris of choice, fall away. Further revealed stands the actual life you have chosen as you have sought to be truly yourself.

What a remarkable freedom! What a remarkable responsibility - to alone be responsible for the path you choose and the consequences, good and bad, that ensue. Some persons rejoice at the freedom to use choice, will, and action to create their very own lives. Others skulk in the shadows of what could be, hoarding possibilities, but never actualizing their own possibilities.

Yes, temperaments may vary, but not the outcome. You can have a life that expresses who you are or you can have instead the reasons why you don't. Either way in the end you will have something. And only you will be responsible for that outcome.

Choice, will, and action express the common understanding of how to act. Yet spiritual teachers speak of another way of moving through the world - non-action. When at last you rest within yourself, as yourself, your actions spring forth as an effortless, spontaneous response to the needs of the moment.

Personal Freedom

The basic step in achieving inward freedom is "choosing one's self." This strange sounding phrase of Kierkegaard's means to affirm one's responsibility for one's self and one's existence. It is the attitude which is opposite to blind momentum or routine existence; it is an attitude of aliveness or decisiveness; it means that one recognizes that he exists in his particular spot in the universe, and he accepts the responsibility for his existence. This is what Nietzsche meant by the "will to live" ~ not simply the instinct for self-preservation, but the will to accept the fact that one is one's self, and to accept responsibility for fulfilling one's destiny, which in turn implies accepting the fact that one must make his basic choices himself.

~ Rollo May (1909-1994)
American existential psychologist and author
in *Man's Search for Himself*

A part of Fate is the freedom of man. Forever wells up the impulse of choosing and acting in his soul.

~ Ralph Waldo Emerson (1803-1882)
American transcendentalist author, poet, and philosopher
in *The Conduct of life*

Freedom is man's capacity to take a hand in his own development.

~ Rollo May (1909-1994)
American existential psychologist and author
in *Man's Search for Himself*

Most people do not really want freedom, because freedom involves responsibility, and most people are frightened of responsibility.

~ Sigmund Freud (1856-1939)
Austrian father of psychoanalysis
in *Civilization and Its Discontents*

This is the highest wisdom that I own... freedom and life are earned by those alone who conquer them each day anew.

~ Johann Wolfgang von Goethe (1749-1832)
German poet, dramatist, novelist, and scientist
in *Goethe's Faust* translated by Walter Kaufmann

Choice

Your life is the sum result of all the choices you make, both consciously and unconsciously. If you can control the process of choosing, you can take control of all aspects of your life. You can find the freedom that comes from being in charge of yourself.

~ Robert Bennett (1933-2011)
United States Senator

A person's looking for a simple truth to live by, there it is. CHOICE. To refuse to passively accept what we've been handed by nature or society, but to choose for ourselves. CHOICE. That's the difference between emptiness and substance, between a life actually lived and a wimpy shadow cast on an office wall.

~ Tom Robbins (1932-present)
American novelist and essayist
in *Still Life with Woodpecker*

It's when we're given choice that we sit with the gods and design ourselves.
~ Dorothy Gilman (1923-present)
American writer

As a man thinketh so is he, and as a man chooseth so is he.

~ Ralph Waldo Emerson (1803-1882)
American transcendentalist author, poet, and philosopher
"Spiritual Laws" in *Essays: First Series*

He is free ... who knows how to keep in his own hands the power to decide, at each step, the course of his life....

~ Salvador de Madariaga y Rojo (1886-1978)
Spanish diplomat, writer, historian and pacifist

Highly proactive people recognize their "response-ability" - the ability to choose their response. They do not blame circumstances, conditions, or conditioning for their behavior. Their behavior is a product of their own conscious choice, based on values, rather than a product of their conditions, based on feeling.

~ Stephen Covey (1932-2012)
American educator, author, businessman
in *The 7 Habits of Highly Effective People*

What man wants is simply independent choice, whatever that independence may cost and wherever it may lead.

~ Fyodor Dostoyevsky (1821–1881)
Russian novelist, essayist, journalist and philosopher
in *Notes from Underground* translated by Constance Garnett

Every man builds his world in his own image. He has the power to choose, but no power to escape the necessity of choice. If he abdicates his power, he abdicates the status of man....

~ Ayn Rand (1905-1982)
Russian-born American author and philosopher
in *Atlas Shrugged*

Alternatives exclude.

~ John Gardner (1933-1982)
American novelist
in *Grendel*

For every yes there must be a no, and every positive choice means you have to relinquish others. Many of us shrink from fully apprehending the limits, diminishment, and loss that are riveted to existence.

~Irvin Yalom (1931-present)
American existential psychiatrist and author
in *Staring at the Sun*

Choosing a path meant having to miss out on others. She had a whole life to live, and she was always thinking that, in the future, she might regret the choices she made now. "I'm afraid of committing myself," she thought to herself. She wanted to follow all possible paths and so ended up following none.

~ Paulo Coelho (1947-present)
Brazilian lyricist and novelist
in *Brida*

You can avoid reality, but you cannot avoid the consequences of avoiding reality.

~ Ayn Rand (1905-1982))
Russian-born American author and philosopher
in *Atlas Shrugged*

Before something can be a full value, it must meet these criteria. It must be:
  chosen freely
  chosen from among alternatives
  chosen after due reflection
  prized and cherished
  publicly affirmed
  acted upon
  part of a pattern that is a repeated action

~ Sidney Simon
contemporary American educator
in *Meeting Yourself Halfway*

Valuing is creating; hear it, ye creating ones! Valuation itself is the treasure and jewel of the valued things.

Through valuation only is there value; and without valuation the nut of existence would be hollow. Hear it ye creating ones!

~ The character of Zarathustra in *Thus Spake Zarathustra*
by Friedrich Nietzsche (1844-1900)
German philosopher

The biblical passage which says of Abraham and the three visiting angels: "And He stood over them under the tree and they did eat" is interpreted by Rabbi Zusya to the effect that man stands above the angels, because he knows something unknown to them, namely, that eating may be hallowed by the eater's intention ... Any natural act, if hallowed, leads to God, and nature needs man for what no angel can perform on it, namely, its hallowing.

~ Martin Buber (1878-1965)
Jewish philosopher
in *The Way of Man: According to the Teaching of Hasidism*

Will

The education of the will is the object of our existence.

~ Ralph Waldo Emerson (1803-1882)
American transcendentalist author, poet, and philosopher
in *Courage*

The magnum opus is pre-eminently the creation of man by himself, that is, the full and complete conquest which he can make of his faculties and his future; it is pre-eminently the perfect emancipation of his will.

by Eliphas Levi (1810-1875)
French occult author and ceremonial magician
cited in *The Mysteries of Magic* by Arthur Waite

Each man is the painter for his own life; the craftsman in this task is the will.

~ Ancient Latin saying by unknown
cited in *Strength of Will* by Edward Boyd Barrett

A man is what he wills himself to be.

~ Jean-Paul Sartre (1905-1980)
French existential philosopher and author
in *No Exit*

Willing emancipateth: that is the true doctrine of will and emancipation - so teacheth you Zarathustra. No longer willing, and no longer valuing, and no longer creating! Ah, that that great debility may ever be far from me! And also in discerning do I feel only my will's procreating and evolving delight ...

~ The character of Zarathustra in *Thus Spake Zarathustra*, by Friedrich Nietzsche (1844-1900)
German philosopher

Will to will! The Will must be: developed, grounded, re-oriented and used!

~ Roberto Assagioli (1888–1974)
Italian psychologist and founder of **Psychosynthesis**
in *The Act of Will*

The act of will consists of six sequential phases or stages. They are:

The Purpose, Aim, or Goal, based on Evaluation, Motivation and Intention.
Deliberation.
Choice and Decision.
Affirmation: the Command, or "Fiat," of the Will.
Planning and Working out a Program.
Direction of the Execution.

~ Roberto Assagioli (1888–1974)
Italian psychologist and founder of Psychosynthesis
in *The Act of Will*

Since the outcome of successful willing is the satisfaction of one's needs, we can see that the act of will is essentially joyous. And the realization of ... being a self ... gives a sense of freedom, of power, of mastery which is profoundly joyous.

~ Roberto Assagioli (1888–1974)
Italian psychologist and founder of Psychosynthesis

Action

Expressing what you are is taking action. You can have a great many ideas in your head, but what makes the difference is the action. Without action upon an idea, there will be no manifestation, no results, and no reward.

~ Don Miguel Ruiz (1952-present)
Mexican author
in *The Four Agreements*

Whatever you think you can do or believe you can do, begin it. Action has magic, grace, and power in it. Begin it now.

~ Johann Wolfgang von Goethe (1749-1832
German poet, dramatist, novelist, and scientist

Knowing is not enough; we must apply. Willing is not enough; we must do.

~ Johann Wolfgang von Goethe (1749-1832
German poet, dramatist, novelist, and scientist

Men must not only know, they must act.

~ W. E. B. Du Bois (1868-1963)
civil rights activist, Pan-Africanist, sociologist, historian

He who desires but acts not, breeds pestilence.

~ William Blake (1757-1827)
British poet
in *The Marriage of Heaven and Hell*

You miss 100 percent of the shots you never take.

~ Wayne Gretzky (1961-present)
Canadian professional ice hockey player

There is no reality except in action.

~ Jean-Paul Sartre (1905-1980)
French existential philosopher and author
in *Existentialism is a Humanism*

Take time to deliberate, but when the time for action comes, stop thinking and go in.

~ Napoleon Bonaparte (1769-1821)
French military and political leader

Action may not always bring happiness, but there is no happiness without action.

~ William James (1842-1910)
American psychologist and philosopher

Action springs not from thought, but from a readiness for responsibility.

~ Dietrich Bonhoeffer (1906-1945)
German Lutheran pastor and theologian
in *Letters & Papers from Prison*

Responsibility

Freedom is the will to be responsible to ourselves.

~ Friedrich Nietzsche (1844-1900)
German philosopher

You and you alone are responsible for the crucial aspects of your life situation, and only you have the power to change it. And even if you face overwhelming external restraints, you will have the freedom and the choice of adopting various attitudes towards those restraints.

~Irvin Yalom (1931-present)
American existential psychiatrist and author
in *Staring at the Sun*

Stand up, be bold, be strong. Take the whole responsibility on your own shoulders, and know that you are the creator of your own destiny. All the strength and succor you want is within yourselves. Therefore, make your own future.

~ Swami Vivekananda (1863-1902)
Indian Hindu monk
in *Pearls of Wisdom*

Taking personal accountability is a beautiful thing because it gives us complete control of our destinies.

~ Heather Schuck
contemporary American author
in *The Working Mom Manifesto*

Man is condemned to be free; because once thrown into the world, he is responsible for everything he does.

~ Jean-Paul Sartre (1905-1980)
French existential philosopher and author
in *Existentialism is a Humanism*

Each man lives for himself, uses his freedom to achieve his personal goals, and feels with his whole being that right now he can or cannot do such-and-such an action; but as soon as he does it, this action, committed at a certain moment in time, becomes irreversible, and makes itself the property of history, in which it has not a free but a predestined significance.

~ Leo Tolstoy (1862-1910)
Russian novelist
in *War and Peace*

One's philosophy is not best expressed in words; it is expressed in the choices one makes ... And the choices we make are ultimately our responsibility.

~ Eleanor Roosevelt (1884-1962)
former first lady of the United States and humanitarian

You need only claim the events of your life to make yourself yours. When you truly possess all you have been and done, which may take some time, you are fierce with reality.

~ Florida Scott-Maxwell (1883-1979)
American psychologist, playwright, and author
in *The Measure of My Days*

I believe that we are solely responsible for our choices, and we have to accept the consequences of every deed, word, and thought throughout our lifetime.

~ Elisabeth Kübler-Ross (1926-2004)
Swiss-American psychiatrist, a pioneer in near-death studies
cited on the Elisabeth Kübler-Ross Foundation website

You choose, you live the consequences. Every yes, no, maybe, creates the school you call your personal experience.

~ Richard Bach (1937-present)
American author
in *Running from Safety*

The natural rights with which We have been dealing are, however, inseparably connected, in the very person who is their subject, with just as many respective duties. And rights as well as duties find their source, their sustenance and their inviolability in the natural law which grants or enjoins them....

For every fundamental human right draws its indestructible moral force from the natural law, which, in granting it, imposes a corresponding obligation. Those, therefore, who claim their own rights, yet altogether forget or neglect to carry out their respective duties, are people who build with one hand and destroy with the other.

~ Pope John XXIII (1881-1963)
in the *Pacem in Terris* encyclical letter

Non-Action

The mystery is this: there is one right thing and only one right thing to do at every moment.

~ Robert A. Johnson (1921-present)
American Jungian analyst and author
in *Balancing Heaven and Earth*

Freedom insists that the ego can do anything it wishes. I do not mean to toss the concept of freedom out entirely. Of course we have free will, but I am insisting that in every moment there is one right thing to do; we can choose to follow the will of God or not follow the will of God, and only in this way can we live meaningful lives.

~ Robert A. Johnson (1921-present)
American Jungian analyst and author
in *Balancing Heaven and Earth*

Devadatta asked; "Wherefrom is each action begun?" The Blessed One answered: "From the most necessary; because each moment contains its necessity and this is called the justice of action."...

A spirited steed even with the end of his hoof feels on which stone to step next. So is felt the order of mobility, co-measurement and necessity.

~ Helena Roerich (1879-1955)
Russian mystic and author
in *Leaves from Morya's Garden II*

So instead of intention one experiences a spontaneous flow of intelligent and purposeful action, realizing that Being flows through one, as one, and it is the flow that determines one's life, action, interests, creativity and so on....

As the Personal Essence, one becomes the spearhead of reality. Reality acts through one by one being the individual manifestation of it. In religious language this is called surrender to God's will, or flowing with the Tao.

~ A. H. Almaas (1944-present)
Kuwaiti-born American psychologist and philosopher
in *The Pearl Beyond Price*

But he that hath the steerage of my course
Direct my sail.

~ The character of Romeo in *Romeo and Juliet*
by William Shakespeare (1564-1616)
English playwright

One who has reached full maturity, who knows himself in consciousness will not necessarily conform with social convention. Such a one will act at the right moment as the situation dictates, without anybody being hindered in any way. If your acts are dictated by your desires, you have no freedom whatsoever. On the other hand, if you do what the situation calls for, you do what is right and you and your surroundings are free.

~ Jean Klein (1916-1998)
French Advaita Vedanta master
in *I Am*

When the I is absent the situation presents itself to you as a collection of facts. When there is no one involved in these facts right action appears spontaneously. Seeing all the facts calls for acceptance. Where there is no longer psychological involvement there are no opposing factors and therefore no choices of some facts, some elements over others. Acceptance does not come from the body-mind, it comes from our wholeness. Once all the elements of the situation are welcomed in our acceptance free from qualifying, the situation itself calls for action, but we do not go to it already armed.

~ Jean Klein (1916-1998)
French Advaita Vedanta master
in *I Am*

When there is a need for action, Being responds, it does not react. Being responds by manifesting a state, a quality that is needed objectively at the moment.

~ A. H. Almaas (1944-present)
Kuwaiti-born American psychologist and philosopher
in *Diamond Heart Book Three: Being and the Meaning of Life*

One who lives in silence is purposeless. He accomplishes whatever must be accomplished. One could say there is spontaneous purposeless activity.

~ Jean Klein (1916-1998)
French Advaita Vedanta master
in *Ease of Being*

The only difference between Adamic man and the man of today is that the one was born to paradise and the other has to create it. And that brings me back to the question of choice. A man can only prove that he is free by electing to be so. And he can only do so when he realizes that he himself made himself unfree. And that to me means that he must wrest from God the powers he has given God. The more of God he recognizes in himself the freer he becomes. And the freer he becomes the fewer decisions he has to make, the less choice is presented to him. Freedom is a misnomer. Certitude is more like it. Unerringness. Because truthfully there is always only one way to act in any situation, not two, nor three.

~ Henry Miller (1891-1980)
American author
in *Big Sur and the Oranges of Hieronymous Bosch*

The actions of the Taoist sage thus arise out of his intuitive wisdom, spontaneously and in harmony with his environment. He does not need to force himself, or anything around him, but merely adapts his actions to the movements of the Tao. In the words of Huai Nan Tzu,

Those who follow the natural order flow in the current of the Tao.

Such a way of acting is called **wu-wei** in Taoist philosophy; a term which means literally 'non-action', and which Joseph Needham translates as 'refraining from activity contrary to nature,' justifying this interpretation with a quotation from the Chuang-tzu,

Non-action does not mean doing nothing and keeping silent. Let everything be allowed to do what it naturally does, so that its nature will be satisfied.

... This is the meaning of Lao Tzu's seemingly so puzzling words, "By non-action, everything can be done."

~ Fritjof Capra (1939-present)
Austrian-born American physicist
in *The Tao of Physics*

9

LIVING IN PROCESS

The most fundamental lesson I have learned about life is this: The essence of my being is that I am subjective awareness continually in process ... I am solely the process of my being.

~ James Bugental (1915-2008)
American psychotherapist and author
in *The Art of the Psychotherapist*

If I were to ask you who are you, you might reply, "Jane" or "John". Typically you probably always think of yourself as an unchanging identity - Jane or John. However, in fact from moment to moment you are never the same person.

How you now know yourself differs greatly from how you knew yourself when you were five years old. Over the years your body has changed, as have your feelings, thoughts, aspirations, and roles. What has not changed? In fact, even your identity has changed, i.e., child, teen, adult, parent.

More precisely, how you experience yourself this moment differs from how you experienced yourself this morning. In fact each instant provides a bounty of new experience, sensations, feelings, and thoughts. How could you be the same unchanging identity?

You and I are not static nouns, we are verbs; we are not things, we are action. We are not experiencers, we are the experienc*ing*. We are psychological and spiritual processes unfolding our uniqueness as individuals through time.

To be yourself, then, is to settle more into the dynamic process that you are. Understanding yourself to be a psycho-spiritual process liberates your aliveness and spontaneity from the fixed identity you might have misunderstood yourself to be.

It is through his understanding of the word "process" that the disciple discovers the true meaning of the occult statement that "before a man can tread the path he must become that Path himself."

~ Alice A. Bailey (1880-1949)
American esotericist
in *The Rays and the Initiations*

Each of us is in a constant state of transformation - of one experience opening up to another, one action leading to another, one perception multiplying into many others; of perception growing into knowledge, knowledge leading to action, and action creating more experience.

~ A. H. Almaas (1944-present)
Kuwaiti-born American psychologist and philosopher
in *Spacecruiser Inquiry*

The "self" in Self Acceptance Training is actually a process. You are not the body, not the ego, but the process. You are what exists right now, not what you were a minute ago or what you will be a minute from now, to say nothing of a year ago or a year from now.

~ Dick Olney (1915-1994)
American human potential therapist
cited in *Walking in Beauty* edited by Roslyn Moore

It is particularly this experience of the self as a flow of Presence in a dynamic unfoldment that we call the soul, the ancient western term for the self.

~ A. H. Almaas (1944-present)
Kuwaiti-born American psychologist and philosopher
in *The Point of Existence*

Life is a process of becoming, a combination of states we have to go through. Where people fail is that they wish to elect a state and remain in it. This is a kind of death.

~ Anais Nin (1903-1977)
French-Cuban author and diarist
cited in iMind: *The Art of Change and Self-Therapy* by David Arnold.

A foolish consistency is the hobgoblin of little minds, adored by little statesmen and philosophers and divines. With consistency a great soul has simply nothing to do ... Speak what you think now in hard words and to-morrow speak what tomorrow thinks in hard words again, though it contradict every thing you said to-day.

~ Ralph Waldo Emerson (1803-1882)
American transcendentalist author, poet, and philosopher
"Self Reliance" in *Essays: First Series*

Let it go. Let it out.
Let it all unravel.
Let it free and it can be
A path on which to travel.

~ Michael Leunig (1945-present)
Australian cartoonist and poet
in *The Travelling Leunig*

I live on Earth at present, and I don't know what I am. I know that I am not a category. I am not a thing -- a noun. I seem to be a verb, an evolutionary process -- an integral function of the universe.

~ Buckminster Fuller (1895-1983)
American philosopher, theorist, architect, and inventor
in *I Seem to be a Verb*

We are, in our deepest nature, processes, not things. We are humans, be-ing. We are the ing of our doing. We are not what we do, but the do-ing. We are not what we think, but the think-ing .... Life, process, is always moving on, always in process.

~ James Bugental (1915-2008)
American existential/humanistic psychotherapist and author
in *The Art of the Psychotherapist*

The most fundamental lesson I have learned about life is this: The essence of my being is that I am subjective awareness continually in process ... I am solely the process of my being - as an example, I am the process of writing these words, but I am not the content of the words or the ideas they express. I am the being aware of writing, the choosing ways of expressing thoughts, the hoping for communication, the enjoying of the emergence in thoughts and images of what I have experienced.

~ James Bugental (1915-2008)
American existential/humanistic psychotherapist and author
in *Search for Identity*

Every person must follow her own process. No one else knows what is right for another. There is no goal in living our process, except to live it. Our processes can change. Our lives can change as we participate in the process. Our only requirement is to trust the process and live in faith. Our responsibility is to live out what our Creator asks of us. To live our lives. Living our process demands a deep spiritual commitment of being one with one's life.

~ Anne Wilson Schaef
contemporary American writer and lecturer
in *Living in Process*

Man is a stream whose source is hidden.... I am constrained every moment to acknowledge a higher origin for events than the will I call mine.

~ Ralph Waldo Emerson (1803-1882)
American transcendentalist author, poet, and philosopher
"The Over-Soul" in *Essays: First Series*

Life will give you whatever experience is most helpful for the evolution of your consciousness. How do you know this is the experience you need? Because this is the experience you are having at the present moment.

~ Eckhart Tolle (1948-present)
German-born spiritual teacher
in *A New Earth*

Situations are the voice of my guru, the presence of my guru.

~ Chogyam Trungpa (1939-1987)
Tibetan meditation master, scholar, and artist
in *Cutting Through Spiritual Materialism*

This very moment is the perfect teacher.

~ Pema Chodron (1936-present)
American Tibetan Buddhist nun
in *When Things Fall Apart*

As you unfold... just keep on, quietly and earnestly, growing through all that happens to you. You cannot disrupt this process more violently than by looking outside yourself for answers that may only be found by attending to your innermost feelings.

~ Rainer Maria Rilke (1875-1926)
Bohemian-Austrian poet and novelis

Only go as fast as your slowest part.

~ Ann Weiser Cornell (1949-present)
American author, educator, worldwide authority on **Focusing**

10

APPROACHES TO PERSONAL TRANSFORMATION

Thou shall bear all things that all things may change.

~ Sri Aurobindo (1872-1950)
Indian philosopher, mystic, poet, and nationalist
in *Savitri*

If you want to change yourself, then by definition you have an idea of how you think you should be. Maybe you want to be more kind, more confident, or more spiritual. So you set forth trying to fit the round peg of who you are into the square hole of your ideal. To better fit your ideal, you shave this part of your personality off, you tweak that part, tap here, hammer there.

Working on yourself in this way, yes, you may achieve a facsimile of your ideal, but you have not become yourself. Rather psychologists would describe your efforts as your seeking to actualize a self-image ideal which is different from actualizing who you are.

Given your interest in being yourself, how then do you become yourself? By being yourself as you are in any moment. What could be more simple! What could be more difficult, given your social conditioning, personal history, and inner critic!

By being yourself as you are, you actualize your wholeness. You cease presumptuous meddling with the natural unfolding of your inner process.

The unconditional embrace of your darkness by the light of your awareness allows the possibility of natural transformation.

As pleasant and unpleasant thoughts, feelings, experiences unfold without interference, you simply accompany your experience, understanding it as best you can. You don't have to force change. The living process that you are ceaselessly evolves naturally.

◊ ◊ ◊

Self-Actualization vs. Self-Image Actualization

We cannot deliberately bring about changes in ourselves or others ... people who do so typically end up dedicating their lives to actualize a concept of what they should be like rather than to actualize themselves. This difference between self-actualizing and self-image actualizing is very important.

~ Fritz Perls (1893-1970)
German-American **gestalt psychologist**

The neurotic process ... is a process of abandoning the real self for an idealized one; of trying to actualize this pseudoself instead of our given human potentials.

~ Karen Horney (1885-1952)
American psychotherapist
in *Neurosis and Human Growth*

"The same thing's happening to you as happened to the crow."
"What happened to the crow, Zorba?"
"Well, you see, he used to walk respectably, properly - well, like a crow. But one day he got it into his head to try and strut about like a

pigeon. And from that time on the poor fellow couldn't for the life of him recall his own way of walking. He was all mixed up, don't you see? He just hobbled about."

~ The character of Zorba speaking to the narrator in *Zorba the Greek* by Nikos Kazantzakis (1883–1957)
Greek author, poet, and philosopher

No man ... can wear one face to himself and another to the multitude without finally getting bewildered as to which may be true.

~ Nathaniel Hawthorne (1804-1864)
American Author
in *The Scarlet Letter*

Similarly, in Christianity, Christ is an exemplar who dwells in every Christian as his integral personality. But historical trends lead to the *imitatio Christi* whereby the individual does not pursue his own destined road to wholeness, but attempts to imitate the way taken by Christ.

~ Carl Jung (1875-1961)
Swiss depth psychologist
in *Memories, Dreams, Reflections*

The relation of personality to suprapersonal values may be achieved either in the realm of objectivization, and this easily gives rise to slavery of man, or in the existential realm, in a process of transcension, in which case life with freedom is born.

~ Nicholas Berdyaev (1874-1948)
Russian **Christian existentialist** philosopher
in *Slavery and Freedom*

There is a time in every man's education when he arrives at the conviction that envy is ignorance; that imitation is suicide; that he must take himself for better or worse as his portion; that though the wide universe is full of good, no kernel of nourishing corn can come to him but through his toil bestowed on that plot of ground which is given him to till. The power which resides in him is new in nature, and none but he knows what that is which he can do, nor does he know until he has tried.

~ Ralph Waldo Emerson (1803-1882)
American transcendentalist author, poet, and philosopher
"Self Reliance" in *Essays: First Series*

"Why not let me be anything? Why should I try to be so religious?"
"I said nothing about religion. Religion means other people are on your path too: They'll drag you down. No, you must be your own person, and you must resist following others' ideals. Filling yourself with the thinking of other people limits you. You must realize your own nature by yourself. Self-disciplinary realization is the key. You say you want to be free to be anything, but you can't. You must only be free to be yourself. You must know yourself, bring what is within yourself to fruition."

~ The character of Grand Master teaching little Butterfly in *The Chronicles of Tao* by Deng Ming-Dao

[Carl Rogers] saw human beings as having a deep need for the respect and appreciation of others, a need which often conflicts with the other felt needs the person has. Such conflict does not itself constitute psychological disturbance, according to Rogers; there is such disturbance only when a person denies or distorts their own felt needs so as to develop a self-concept which fits the 'conditions of worth' of those around them.

~ Campbell Purton
contemporary English experiential psychotherapist
in *Person-Centered Therapy*

If one is greedy, envious, or violent, it takes honesty to know, to understand, that one is greedy, envious, or violent. To pursue an ideal of non-greed, non-violence, away from 'what is', is, in fact, an escape which prevents one from discovering and acting directly upon what one is. To understand this obvious fact needs an extraordinary perception.

The understanding of what one is, without distortion, is the beginning of virtue - whatever one is, ugly or beautiful, wicked or mischievous. And virtue gives freedom. It is only in virtue that one can live, one can discover 'what-is'. But it must be clearly understood, again, that there is a basic difference between being virtuous and becoming virtuous.

Being virtuous comes from the understanding of 'what-is', whereas becoming virtuous - cultivation of virtue - means covering up 'what-is' with what one would like to be.

~ Ramesh Balsekar (1917-2009)
Indian Advaita Vedanta teacher
in *The Only Way to Live*

If someone is guiding you, that is suspicious, because you are relying on something external. Being fully what you are in yourself becomes guidance.

~ Chogyam Trungpa (1939-1987)
Tibetan meditation master, scholar, and artist
in *Cutting Through Spiritual Materialism*

What the superior man seeks is in himself. What the mean man seeks is in others.

~ Confucius (551–479 BCE)
Chinese philosopher
in *The Confucian Analects*

To be as good as someone else is no high ideal. I am myself.

~ Paul Robeson (1898-1976)
American actor, singer, athlete, civil rights advocate
cited in *The Undiscovered Paul Robeson* by Paul Robeson Jr.

Once we accept fully and completely exactly who and what we are, we have then given up the struggle to 'be someone else.'

~ Fritz Perls (1893-1970)
German-American gestalt psychologist

Letting Be

To me there is no liberation *a tout prix*. I cannot be liberated from anything I do not possess, have not done or experienced. Real liberation becomes possible for me only when I have done all that I was able to do, when I have completely devoted myself to a thing and participated in it to the utmost. If I withdraw from participation, I am virtually amputating the corresponding part of my psyche. Naturally, there may be good reasons for my not immersing myself in a given experience. But then I am forced to confess my inability, and must know that I may have neglected to do something of vital importance. In this way I make amends for the lack of a positive act by the clear knowledge of my incompetence.

A man who has not passed through the inferno of his passions has never overcome them. They then dwell in the house next door, and at any moment a flame may dart out and set fire to his own house. Whenever we give up, leave behind, and forget too much, there is always the danger that the things we have neglected will return with added force.

~ Carl Jung (1875-1961)
Swiss depth psychologist
in *Memories, Dreams, Reflections*

The problem is that an unintegrated response repeats itself until integrated. On this point, nature seems eternally patient and forever cruel. It may take years or even generations, but a negative experience returns until human presence is brought to touch it with love and acceptance and integrate it.

~ Stephen Gilligan
contemporary American psychotherapist and author
in *The Courage to Love*

A tree reaching up to heaven must have roots reaching down to hell.

~ Friedrich Nietzsche (1844-1900)
German philosopher

As a poisonous substance does not injure the worm born in that substance, so he who does even an unpleasant duty ordained by his own dharma incurs no evil. That is the only real thing for him. All other duties are alien to his nature. Throughout all of Sri Krishna's exhortation to **Arjuna** about duty it should not be forgotten that duty must be performed as an act of worship. From our work we must not seek any personal gain; we must regard ourselves only as instruments for the fulfillment of divine purpose. For Arjuna, participation in the cruel battle is more desirable than the life of a recluse living on alms and inflicting no injury on others. Such a life would be entirely alien to Arjuna's inborn nature.

~ Swami Nikhilananda (1895-1973)
Hindu Swami
in *The Bhagavad Gita* translated by Swami Nikhilananda

The only way out is through.

~ Fritz Perls (1893-1970)
father of gestalt psychologist
cited in *Fat is a Family Affair* by Judi Hollis, American author

All this talk of goodness and duty, these perpetual pinpricks, unnerve and irritate the hearer; nothing, indeed could be more destructive of his inner tranquility. If you indeed want the men of the world not to lose the qualities that are natural to them, you had best study how it is that Heaven and Earth maintain their eternal course...thus you too shall lean to follow the course that the Way of Nature sets; and soon you will reach a goal where you will no longer need to go round laboriously advertising goodness and duty, like the town-crier with his drum, seeking for news of a lost child. No, Sir! What you are doing is to disjoint men's natures!

~ Chuang Tzu (399 BC-295 BC)
Chinese Taoist philosopher
cited in *Crazy Wisdom* by Wes Nisker

'Self-Liberation', in the **Zogqen** sense, means that whatever manifests in the field of experience of the practitioner is allowed to arise just as it is, without judgment of it as good or bad, beautiful or ugly. And in that same moment, if there is no clinging, or attachment, without effort, or even volition, whatever it is that arises, whether as a thought or as a seemingly external event, automatically liberates itself, by itself, and of itself. Practicing in this way the seeds of the poison tree of dualistic vision never even get a chance to sprout, much less to take root and grow.

So the practitioner lives his or her life in an ordinary way, without needing any rules other than his own awareness, but always remaining in the state of primordial unity by integrating his state with whatever arises as part of his experience, and with absolutely nothing to be seen outwardly to show that he is practicing.

~ Namkhai Norbu (1938-present)
Tibetan Buddhist Dzogchen Master
in *The Crystal and the Way of Light*

The moment you try to direct your inner process -- "I should not feel that way, I should feel this way; I want to feel this instead of that" -- you are acting on your belief that you know what you are supposed to experience in the next moment. All ego activity involves this principle.

You might for instance, sense into your inner experience and realize that you are feeling irritated. The moment you say to yourself, "I must let go of it so that I can feel peaceful," you are acting on a plan based on the belief that you should be feeling peaceful. Whenever you attempt to change what you are experiencing, you are assuming that you know what ought to be happening, which indicates that you have a plan in mind. This plan is not necessarily conscious, but it is an implicit part of your inner activity whenever you manipulate, judge, or criticize what you are experiencing.... If instead of trying to manipulate our experience, we stay present with it and try to understand it in an experiential way, then our process unfolds.

~ A. H. Almaas (1944-present)
Kuwaiti-born American psychologist and philosopher
in *Facets of Unity*

It is not necessary to judge thoughts and experiences as good or bad, as desirable or undesirable, profitable or unprofitable. Let them come and go just as they are, without becoming overly involved, without identifying with anything, neither indulging in them by following after them nor suppressing or inhibiting them. Simply let all inner and outer things appear and disappear in their own way, just like clouds in the sky, and remain above and beyond it all, even amidst one's daily activities and responsibilities.

~ Nyoshul Khenpo (1932-2001)
Tibetan Buddhist Dzogchen master
in *Natural Great Perfection*

"Shamunatha was a Great **Tantric** Master. The Way of Tantric Buddhism is the Way of Acceptance, the way of working with all the energies and powers of living, refusing and denying none of them, but using all of them, transforming all of them into wisdom. That is why he is shown surrounded by living things. His is a mind, we say, that makes the world flower; his is a mind that has denied nothing and transformed everything within him and within the world into harmony and spiritual power. This is the way of **Tantra**. It is the hardest way."

"Why?"

"Because it is the most dangerous. Because it has so many temptations --to hedonism, to the relish of worldly power. It is also the most effective way. The man who can travel it successfully, we believe, can attain Enlightenment in one lifetime."

~ Nawang, a Tibetan Monk speaking with the author in *A Journey in Ladakh* by Andrew Harvey

Man cannot approach the divine by reaching beyond the human: he can approach Him through becoming human. To become human is what he, this individual man, has been created for.

~ Martin Buber (1878-1965)
Jewish philosopher
in *Hasidism and Modern Man*

The curious paradox of life is that when I accept myself just as I am, then I can change.

~ Carl Rogers (1902-1987
American psychologist
in *On Becoming a Person*

Part Two:

Becoming Your Self

11

THE VEIL OF THOUGHT

Spiritual awakening is awakening from the dream of thought.

~ Eckhart Tolle (1948-present)
German-born spiritual teacher
in *Stillness Speaks*

Perhaps you wonder, what does thought have to do with learning how to truly be myself in an individual way? It's simple. Your thoughts resemble sunglasses. What you think colors how you see yourself and the world. If you're looking through sunglasses, you're vision is tinted; you're not seeing things as they are.

Usually persons confuse what they think for who they are. But, consider that research suggests we think anywhere from 20,000 - 50,000 thoughts a day! If you multiply that by the number of days in a year and the number of years you have lived, you get a sense of how changing your thoughts are.

But throughout your days your sense of "I" has always remained constant. How could this be so, unless the self you seek to become rests somewhere deeper than your thoughts? Yes, you have thoughts, but you are not your thoughts.

This line of thinking steers the understanding of what it means to be authentic deeper than what is commonly understood in the West. This section and the next address this understanding of what might be called "deep authenticity", where striving to be yourself becomes ultimately fulfilled in the simplicity of your just being as you are in each moment.

To rest in that simplicity, incessant thoughts need to quiet. Like a stick that stirs the bottom of a pond, and clouds the water, thoughts muddy our direct experience of life. Remove the stick and the water settles. Remove the thoughts, and the mind settles, allowing you to peer into the veiled depths.

At this level of understanding, being yourself becomes indistinguishable from resting in your true nature which spiritual traditions have addressed throughout the ages. The concerns of psychology and spirituality become blended, as if two poles of the spectrum of human experience.

Certainly thinking is necessary to function when we are called to function. But when not called to function, we need not go through daily life thinking all the time. Inner silence lifts the veil to reveal the hidden.

The Mind is the great Slayer of the Real. Let the Disciple slay the Slayer.

~ H. P. Blavatsky (1831-1891)
Russian mystic and co-founder of the **Theosophical** Society
in *The Voice of the Silence*

The life of the spirit comes from the prior death of the mind. If people can kill the mind, the original comes alive.

~ Lu Dong Bin (796-?)
Chinese scholar and poet
in *The Secret of the Golden* Flower translated by Thomas Cleary

Two thousand years ago, Mahayana Buddhists said that the structure of our conditioned experience is shaped by the concepts we use to cut the universe up into self and the world, and then we fill these in and make meaning out of our existence. According to Buddhist philosophers, the manifest universe exists as a function of linguistic designation. It comes into being through the distinctions we make and share in language.

~ Peter Fenner (1937-present)
Australian Buddhist scholar and nondual teacher
in *Radiant Mind*

Only when one severs the very root of the mind with the weapon of non-conceptualisation, can one reach the absolute **Brahman** which is omnipresent, supreme peace. Conceptualisation or imagination is productive of error and sorrow; and it can be so easily got rid of by self-knowledge - and when it is got rid of there is great peace.

~ Vasistha (unknown)
Indian Hindu **rishi**
in *Vasistha's Yoga* translated by Swami Venkatsesananda

Give up those erroneous thoughts leading to false distinctions! There is no 'self' and no 'other'. There is no 'wrong desire', no 'anger', no 'hatred', no 'love, no ' victory, no 'failure'. Only renounce the error of intellectual or conceptual thought-processes and your nature will exhibit its pristine purity--for this alone is the way to attain Enlightenment, to observe the Dharma (Law), to become a Buddha and all the rest.

~ Huang Po (d. 850)
Chinese Zen Master
"Wan Ling Record 26" in *The Zen Teachings of Huang Po: On the Transmission of Mind* translated by John Blofeld and P'ei Hsiu

Words and thoughts are invariably dualistic, but pure experience is always nondualistic.

~ Richard Rohr (1943-present)
Franciscan friar and author
in *The Naked Now*

Our understanding here is not that representational thinking is the problem, but that the problem is using representations for perception. To think and speak we have to use representations, but that by itself does not necessarily distort reality. However, when our representations completely determine the ways in which we perceive reality then that becomes a specific problem.

~ A. H. Almaas (1944-present)
Kuwaiti-born American psychologist and philosopher
in *The Void*

You cannot escape your own attitudes, for they will form the nature of what you see. Quite literally you see what you want to see; and you see your own thoughts and emotional attitudes materialized in physical form.

~ Jane Roberts (1929-1984)
American author and spirit medium
in *The Nature of Personal Reality*

We don't see things as they are, we see things as we are.

~ Anais Nin (1903-1977)
French-Cuban author and diarist

The internal dialogue is what grounds people in the daily world. The world is such and such or so and so, only because we talk to ourselves about its being such or such and so and so. The passageway into the world of shamans opens up after the warrior has learned to shut off his internal dialogue.

~ Carlos Castaneda (1925-1998)
Peruvian-born American anthropologist and author
in *Tales of Power*

The single most vital step on your journey toward enlightenment is this: learn to disidentify from your mind. Every time you create a gap in the stream of mind, the light of your consciousness grows stronger.

~ Eckhart Tolle (1948-present)
German-born spiritual teacher
in *The Power of Now: A Guide to Spiritual Enlightenment*

So freedom is not a matter of having one's autonomous mind, it is not a matter of freedom of mind, it is, rather, a matter of freedom from mind.

~ A. H. Almaas (1944-present)
Kuwaiti-born American psychologist and philosopher
in *The Point of Existence*

The mind should be kept independent of any thoughts that arise within it.

~ Gautama Buddha (c. 563 BCE-483 BCE)
in *The Wisdom of Buddhism* by Christian Humphreys

Just pause thought. In that space, do you disappear? What is there in that space? Obviously you are there. You are quite present and aware. That is all. You are, and you know you are. There is both the sense of being or presence and a knowing capacity. Is that awareness 'over there' while you are 'here', or are you that which is aware? Realize that you must be the presence of awareness that remains in the gap between thoughts.

~ John Wheeler
contemporary American nondualist teacher
in *The Light Behind Consciousness*

When understanding dawns, conceptualization ceases and mind becomes vacant. The very nature of the mind is ignorance and therefore stupidity. When the mind stops (conceptualization ceases), peace or wisdom prevails. No thought of either happiness or unhappiness diverts the equanimity of the pure mind.

~ Ramesh Balsekar (1917-2009)
Indian Advaita Vedanta master
in *The Final Truth*

Rama, in the scriptures words have been used in order to facilitate the imparting of instruction. Cause and effect, the self and the Lord, difference and non-difference, knowledge and ignorance, pain and pleasure - all these pairs have been invented for the instruction of the ignorant. They are not real in themselves. All this discussion and argumentation takes place only in and because of ignorance; when there is knowledge there is no duality. When the truth is known, all descriptions cease, and silence alone remains.

~ Vasistha (unknown)
Indian Hindu rishi
in *Vasistha's Yoga* translated by Swami Venkatsesananda

Fast from thoughts, fast:
Thoughts are like the lion and the wild beasts;
People's hearts are the thickets they haunt.

~ Jalal ad-Din Muhammad Rumi (1207-1273)
Persian poet and Sufi master
cited in *The Knowing Heart* translated by Kabir Helminski

Step aside from all thinking, and there is nowhere you can't go.

~ Seng-ts'an (?-606)
the Third Founding Teacher of Zen
cited in *Loving What Is* by Byron Katie

Love has befriended Hafiz so completely.
It has turned to ash and freed me
of every concept and image my mind has ever known.

~ Hafiz (c. 1310-1406)
Persian poet and Sufi master
cited in *The Wonder of Being* by John Wheeler

In order for innate awareness to reveal itself, "Without projecting or concentrating, remain free of discursive thought."

~ Patrul Rinpoche (1808-1887)
Tibetan Buddhist teacher and author
"The Three Incisive Precepts" in *The Flight of the Garuda* by Keith Dowman

12

THE SELF

Your duty is to be; and not to be this or that.

~ Ramana Maharshi (1879-1950)
Hindu guru
in *Talks with Sri Ramana Maharshi*

At the moment of birth, you exist, although without the many things which persons use to identify who they are: name, identity, role in life, memories, etc. You simply are.

From that moment on, life presents you with a ceaseless river of experience, sensations, feelings, thoughts, and even identities which you come to believe you are. But are you really? Take a closer look.

Every moment *is* change. You cannot be what you experience, because although your experience always changes, your sense of "I" remains the same..

From infant to toddler to pre-school, primary, junior, high school, college, and on, each day you experience many changing feelings. Who you are cannot be your feelings, for although they change you experience of "I" is constant.

Researchers now suggest that each day you may think tens of thousands of thoughts. How could you think you are your thoughts, when amid the myriad of fleeting thoughts your sense of yourself as "I" never changes?

Maybe you think you are your identity as mother, father, daughter, son, teacher, business person, etc. Yet over a lifetime your identity changes many times, but the sense of "I" does not.

Yes you have an identity, but *you* are not your identity. Yes you have thoughts, feelings, sensations, and experiences, but *you* are not these.

Then who are you? Well, who were you at the moment of birth before you acquired experiences, sensations, feelings, thoughts, and identities?

You were and you are a profound presence with an innate sense of "I". Your presence has an inherent sense that you exist. Can you deny that you exist?

Your presence also has an intrinsic sense of knowing, an awareness that makes possible the knowing of each moment's experience. Some traditions liken this awareness to an open sky through which pass your thoughts, feelings, sensations, and experiences. Yes, your sky-like awareness experiences these, but is not these.

Where the existential view of personal authenticity culminates in the cultivation of your individuality, the spiritual view culminates in your realization of and your resting in this presence which has been called the Self, awareness, consciousness, Being, etc.

How curious that when just resting in Being, you are most easily yourself, free to spontaneously be just as you are in each moment. Is not that ease the culmination of learning how to be yourself?

The path to personal authenticity removes the hindrances without and the obscurations within which prevent you from just simply being as you are.

Always this freedom to simply be yourself dwells within you, awaiting your discovery once you answer the call to your own authentic life.

Hidden Splendor

TRUTH is within ourselves; it takes no rise
From outward things, whate'er you may believe.
There is an inmost centre in us all,
Where truth abides in fullness; and around,
Wall upon wall, the gross flesh hems it in,
This perfect, clear perception - which is truth.
A baffling and perverting carnal mesh
Binds it, and makes all error: and to KNOW
Rather consists in opening out a way
Whence the imprisoned splendour may escape,
Than in effecting entry for a light
Supposed to be without.

~ Robert Browning (1812-1889)
English poet
in *Paracelsus*

The kingdom of Heaven is within you.

~ Jesus of Nazareth (7–2 BC to 30–33 AD)

Turn into yourself; truth dwells within man.

~ St. Augustine of Hippo (354-430)
Christian Church Father

To spell out only one implication here, these propositions affirm the existence of the higher values within human nature itself, to be discovered there.

~ Abraham Maslow (1908-1970)
American psychologist
in *Towards a Psychology of Being*

You do not need to work to become spiritual. You *are* spiritual.

~ Julia Cameron (1948-present)
American teacher, author
in *God is No Laughing Matter*

For within you is the light of the world--the only light that can be shed upon the Path. If you are unable to perceive it within you, it is useless to look for it elsewhere.

~ Mabel Collins (1851-1927)
English Theosophist
in *Light on the Path*

If you cannot find the truth where you are, where do you expect to find it?

~ Dogen Zenji (1200-1253)
Japanese Zen Buddhist Master

After his great awakening beneath the bodhi tree in Bodhgaya, Lord Buddha said that the ultimate nature of mind is perfectly pure, profound, quiescent, luminous, uncompounded, unconditioned, unborn and undying, and free since the beginningless beginning... This is our birthright, our true nature. It is not something missing, to be sought for and obtained, but is the very heart of our original existential being.

~ Nyoshul Khenpo (1932-2001)
Tibetan Buddhist Dzogchen master
in *Natural Great Perfection*

When one realizes the natural state, the true nature of all beings, there is naturally a welling up of inconceivable spontaneous compassion, loving-kindness, consideration, and empathy, because one realizes there is no self separate from others.

~ Nyoshul Khenpo (1932-2001)
Tibetan Buddhist Dzogchen master
in *Natural Great Perfection*

Gods, heavens, paths, practices, techniques, ethics and so on, are all created by the mind that is under the impression that reality is far away. For the one who sees this light in himself, there is no law or rule – just love, which is the natural expression of your heart when ignorance and suffering are no more. Even that is too much really. There is just what is, as it is. Everything just shines in the light of awareness and everything is settled.

~ John Wheeler
contemporary American nondualist teacher
in *Awakening to the Natural State*

Awareness / Consciousness / Being

Like a fish that does not realize it lives in water because water is the only medium it has ever known, some things are so obvious that they escape our understanding. For human beings, awareness is the "water" in which we always live, yet few of us are taught to recognize and understand our own experience of being aware.

~ Richard Moss MD
contemporary American spiritual teacher
in *The Mandala of Being*

Do you hold a mirror in front of you to know your own Being? The awareness is the "I." Realize it and that is the truth.

~ Ramana Maharshi (1879-1950)
Hindu guru
in *Talks with Ramana Maharshi* by Sri Munagala Venkataramiah

What you are looking for is what is looking

~ St. Francis of Assisi (c. 1181-1226)
Italian Catholic friar and preacher

So it is clear from our own intimate and direct experience that 'I' am not just *present* but am also *aware*. It is for this reason that our self is sometimes referred to as awareness, which simply means the presence of that which is aware…. It is also sometimes referred to as 'consciousness' or 'being'. But most simply this aware presence is known as 'I.'

~ Rupert Spira (1960-present)
English spiritual teacher and writer
in *Presence: The Art of Peace and Happiness Vol. 1*

What we generally call our "personality" is actually memory, a localization for the "I"-image, a shelter to preserve the ego. The moment you identify with the personality, it becomes static, crystallized, and loses all flexibility. But in stepping out of this identification, you take your position in spaceless awareness and the real personality emerges.

~ Jean Klein (1916-1998)
French Advaita Vedanta master
in *Ease of Being*

The life force and the mind are operating, but the mind will tempt you to believe that it is "you." Therefore, understand always that you are the timeless, spaceless witness. And even if the mind tells you that you are the one who is acting, don't believe the mind. Always keep your identity separate from that which is doing the working, thinking and talking..

~ Nisargadatta Maharaj (1897-1981)
Indian guru of Shiva Advaita nondualism
in *Prior to Consciousness: Talks with Sri Nisargadatta Maharaj*

That which *experiences*, on the other hand, is known by many names: the "kingdom of heaven" or "kingdom of God," the "light," "Sophia or "Wisdom," the "Word or "Logos," and *nous* (A Greek word usually translated as "mind" but actually meaning something more like "consciousness"). All these terms reveal different aspects of this primordial Self, or experiencer... the "I" or the "true 'I.'"

~ Richard Smoley (1956-present)
American author, philosopher
in *Inner Christianity: A Guide to the Esoteric Tradition*

222233322222222

222

2

Some call this Quantum Intelligence, God or Allah, some Buddha Mind, or the Tao, others call it Self or Brahman... A spiritual core of awareness within our consciousness that is intrinsically pure, changeless, unconditioned, and free. It is our own presence of awareness that exists in a default mode of perceiving. It can't be damaged or improved.... It's not something you possess, but rather it is who you actually are.

~ Jackson Peterson
contemporary spiritual teacher
in *The Natural Bliss of Being*

Being is the eternal, ever-present One Life beyond the myriad forms of life that are subject to birth and death. However, Being is not only beyond but also deep within every form as its innermost invisible and indestructible essence. This means it is accessible to you now as your own deepest self, your true nature. But don't seek to grasp it with your mind. Don't try to understand it. You can only know it when your mind is still. When you are present, when your attention is fully and intensely in the Now, being can be felt, but it can never be understood mentally. To regain awareness of Being and to abide in that state of "feeling-realization" is enlightenment.

~ Eckhart Tolle (1948-present)
German-born spiritual teacher
in *The Power of Now: A Guide to Spiritual Enlightenment*

: We mostly spend (our scattered lives) conjugating three verbs: to Want, to Have, and to Do. Craving, clutching, and fussing, on the material, political, social, emotional, intellectual - even on the religious - plane, we are kept in perpetual unrest forgetting that none of these verbs have any ultimate significance, except as far as they are transcended by and included in the fundamental verb, to Be: and that Being, not wanting, having and doing, is the essence of a spiritual life.

~ Evelyn Underhill (1875-1941)
English writer
in *The Spiritual Life*

This mysterious existence which comes out of nothing. And you know we don't know how it does. So have reverence, have humility, have gratitude, have respect, and abide in being. Abide in awareness. Abide in existence. I've asked many enlightened people, "What's enlightenment? What is it?"

Until I actually got it. It is just resting in awareness. Resting in existence, resting in being.

~ Deepak Chopra (1947-present)
Indian-born American author and public speaker

GLOSSARY

Abraxas – An Egyptian god who integrates all opposites. In the given context, Abraxas combines good and evil behavior into one godhead.

Advaita Vedanta – A nondual (see "nondual") school of Hinduism. It posits that the true self or Atman is pure awareness. Similarly, the ground of reality or Brahman also is pure awareness.

Arjuna – The protagonist of the Hindu bible, the *Mahabharata*. He represents the everyman who on the battlefield of life is torn between the pairs of opposites with respect to how to conduct life.

Bioenergetic analysis – A somatic or body-oriented psychotherapy modality founded by Alexander Lowen, M.D.

Bodhicitta – A Buddhist term that refers to the attitude that aspires to the welfare and enlightenment of all fellow beings.

Bodhisattva – A Mahayana Buddhist practitioner who has taken the Bodhisattva vow to become enlightened for the sake of all fellow beings.

Brahman – The pure consciousness which Hindus believe is ground of being or Absolute.

Chan – A Mahayana Buddhist school which originated in China.

Christian existentialism – A Christian theological movement which integrates the existential (see "existential") philosophical view.

Dharma – An Eastern term which in this book conveys multiple meanings including the way as taught by the Buddha, right conduct of life, and the law of one's unique being.

Dharmata – The "suchness" of existence as it unfolds in each present moment.

Dzogchen – A Tibetan Buddhist path of spiritual development. Translated as "Natural Perfection", Dzogchen guides its practitioners to experience the natural state of pure awareness which underlies all experience..

Esotericism – Refers to that branch of spiritual knowledge thought to be "hidden" within the dogma of religious institutions.

Existential - A late 19th- and 20th-century philosophical movement which concerned itself with the human subject and its encounter with the conditions of existence.

Focusing – a therapeutic process developed by philosopher Eugene Gendlin.

Fourth Way – A school of spiritual transformation founded by G. I. Gurdjieff which seeks to awaken man from the metaphorical state of "sleep".

Freemasonry – A worldwide fraternal organization whose roots stem from stonemason guilds of the late fourteenth century.

George Ivanovich Gurdjieff – A spiritual teacher of the 20th century who founded a school of spiritual development known as "The Fourth Way" (see Fourth Way).

Gestalt psychology – Understands that the mind self-organizes perceptions and cognitions into meaningful wholes or "gestalts".

Guru Rinpoche – Referring to Padmasambhava (meaning lotus-born), is an expression of Amitabha Buddha.

Hasidic Judaism – A mystical sect of Orthodox Judaism.

Humanism – A philosophical view which values the human person, and esteems critical thinking more than religious doctrine.

Jnani – One who knows, in this context one who knows true nature from personal realization.

Jungian psychology – A psychological school founded by Swiss psychiatrist Carl Gustav Jung. The school especially values the individual psyche and psychological wholeness.

Locus of control – A psychological term which here refers to whether the individual considers the authority over his life to be external to him or within him.

Nasrudin – In this context, a teaching device of the Sufi (see "Sufi") sect of Islam. Nasrudin is a holy fool whose humorous foibles and situations are recounted in many tales which teach spiritual truths.

Nondualism – Also called **non-duality**, refers to the spiritual view that the nature of all existence is "not two" but rather a unity, perhaps pure consciousness, which underlies all appearances.

Psychosynthesis – A school of psychological development founded in the mid-20th century by Italian psychiatrist Roberto Assagioli. The school taught the individual's integration or synthesis of his spiritual and personality, and the integration of the individual into the socio-cultural whole.

Pure Land Buddhism – A school of Mahayana Buddhism whose teachings are based upon Amitabha Buddha.

Rigpa – A Tibetan Dzogchen term which refers to the pure awareness which underlies human experience and all existence.

Rishi is a term for one of the seven inspired poets of the Rig Veda scriptures of ancient Hinduism who were considered sages or saints.

Rudra – A god of the Rig Vedas commonly associated with the turbulent and frightening forces natural forces.

Stoicism – An ancient Greek philosophical school which believed that the perfected person or sage did not experience destructive emotions which were thought to be based upon errors in judgment.

Sufism – The mystical sect of Islam.

Tantra – A Hindu or Buddhist scripture typically associated with more esoteric (see "esotericism") practices.

Tantric – see Vajrayana.

Taoism – An ancient Chinese philosophical school which believes that the tao or "way" is to live in harmony with nature and the inconceivable source which underlies all existence.

Theosophical Society – Founded in 1873, the Society promotes theosophy, an esoteric (see "esotericism") tradition that promotes the individual's personal knowledge of the mysteries of existence.

Transcendentalism – An early 19th century American movement which believed in the goodness of persons and nature.

Vajrayāna – also known as Tantric Buddhism, is a complex and multifaceted system of Buddhist thought and practice which evolved over several centuries.

Wu wei – Literally "non-action", a Taoist (see "Taosim") term that refers to the entirely spontaneous, uncontrived action of the individual who lives in harmony with the Tao. Because the action is sourced by the Tao, there is 'no one' who authors it..

Zogqen – see Dzogchen.

BIBLIOGRAPHY

Some of the authors whom you have read may have inspired you to learn more. You'll find below more information about the sources from which their quotations were taken. Publishers are listed for the print version of the book.

Almaas, A. H. *Being and the Meaning of Life: Diamond Heart Book Three.* Shambhala, 2000. Kindle edition available.

Almaas, A. H. *Diamond Heart Book Four: Indestructible Innocence.* Shambhala, 2000. Kindle edition available.

Almaas, A. H. *Diamond Heart Book Five: Inexhaustible Mystery.* Shambhala, 2011. Kindle edition available.

Almaas, A. H. *Essence: The Diamond Approach to Inner Realization.* Red Wheel Weiser, 1986. Kindle edition available.

Almaas, A. H. *Facets of Unity: The Enneagram of Holy Ideas.* Shambhala, 2000. Kindle edition available.

Almaas, A. H. *The Pearl Beyond Price: Integration of Personality into Being: An Object Relations Approach.* Shambhala, 2000. Kindle edition available.

Almaas, A. H. *The Point of Existence: Transformations of Narcissism in Self-Realization.* Shambhala, 2000. Kindle edition available.

Almaas, A. H. *Spacecruiser Inquiry: True Guidance for the Inner Journey.* Shambhala, 2012. Kindle edition available.

Almaas, A. H. *The Void: Inner Spaciousness and Ego Structure.* Shambhala, 2000. Kindle edition available.

Arden, Harvey & Steve Wall. *Wisdomkeepers: Meetings with Native American Spiritual Elders.* Beyond Words Publishing, 1990.

Arnold, David. *iMind: The Art of Change and Self-Therapy.* AuthorHouse, 2011. Kindle edition available.

Arnold, Matthew. *The Complete Poems.* Lexicos Publishing, 2012. Kindle edition available.

Assagioli, Roberto. *The Act of Will.* The Synthesis Center Inc., 2010.

Attwater, Donald. *Modern Christian Revolutionaries: The Lives and Thought of Kierkegaard - Eric Gill - G.K. Chesterton - C.F. Andrews - Berdyaev.* Devin-Adair Company, 1947.

Bach, Richard. *Running from Safety: An Adventure of the Spirit.* Delta, 1995. Kindle edition available.

Bacon, Francis. *Novum Organum.* Leopold Classic Library, 2015. Kindle edition available.

Bailey, Alice A. *The Labours of Hercules: An Astrological Interpretation.* Lucis Publishing, 2011.

Bailey, Alice A. *The Rays and the Initiations.* Lucis Publishing Company, 1993. Kindle edition available.

Balsekar, Ramesh. *Consciousness Speaks: Conversations with Ramesh S. Balsekar.* Advaita Press, 1992. Kindle edition available.

Balsekar, Ramesh. *The Final Truth: A Guide to Ultimate Understanding.* Advaita Press, 1989. Kindle edition available.

Balsekar, Ramesh. *The Only Way to Live.* Yogi Impressions Books Pvt Ltd, 2007. Kindle edition available.

Barks, Coleman. *The Essential Rumi.* HarperOne, 2004. Kindle edition available.

Barrett, Edward Boyd. *Strength of Will.* Nabu Press, 2012. Kindle edition available.

Berdyaev, Nicholas. *Slavery and Freedom.* Semantron Press, 2009

Blake, William. *William Blake: The Complete Poems.* Penguin, 2004. Kindle edition available.

Blau, Evelyne. *Krishnamurti: 100 Years.* Stewart Tabori & Chang, 1995.

Blavatsky, Helena P. *The Secret Doctrine.* Tarcher, 2009. Kindle edition available.

Blavatsky, Helena P. *The Voice of the Silence.* Theosophical Univ Pr, 1992. Kindle edition available.

Blofeld, John and P'ei Hsiu. *The Zen Teaching of Huang Po: On the Transmission of Mind.* Grove Press, 1994. Kindle edition available.

Bonhoeffer, Dietrich. *Letters & Papers from Prison.* Touchstone, 1997. Kindle edition available.

Branden, Nathaniel. *Taking Responsibility: Self-Reliance and the Accountable Life.* Touchstone, 1997.

Browning, Robert. *Robert Browning's Works.* Seng Books, 2014. Kindle edition available.

Buber, Martin. *Hasidism and Modern Man*. Humanities Press International, 1988.

Buber, Martin. *Tales of the Hasidim: The Early Masters*. Shocken Books, 1961.

Buber, Martin. *The Way of Man: According to the Teaching of Hasidism*. Citadel, 2000. Kindle edition available.

Bugental, James T. *The Search for Existential Identity: Patient-Therapist Dialogues in Humanistic Psychotherapy*. Jossey-Bass, 1976.

Bugental, James T. *The Art of the Psychotherapist: How to Develop Skills that Take Psychotherapy Beyond Science*. W. W. Norton & Company, 1992.

Bugental, James T. *The Search for Authenticity: An Existential-Analytic Approach to Psychotherapy*. Irvington Pub, 1981.

Buscaglia, Leo. *Love: What Life is All About*. Ballantine Books, 1996.

Cameron, Julia.*God is No Laughing Matter*: Observations and Objections on the Spiritual Path. Jeremy P Tarcher , 2001. Kindle edition available.

Cameron, Julia. *Transitions: Prayers and Declarations for a Changing Life*. Jeremy P Tarcher , 1999. Kindle edition available.

Campbell, Joseph. *Creative Mythology*. Penguin Books, 1991.

Campbell, Joseph. *The Power of Myth*. Anchor, 1991. Kindle edition available.

Capra, Fritjof. *The Tao of Physics: An Exploration of the Parallels between Modern Physics and Eastern Mysticism*. Shambhala, 2010. Kindle edition available.

Castaneda, Carlos. *Tales of Power*. Washington Square Press, 1991. Kindle edition available.

Chodron, Pema. *When Things Fall Apart: Heart Advice for Difficult Times*. Shambhala, 2000. Kindle edition available.

Cleary, Thomas. Trans. *The Secret of the Golden Flower*. HarperOne, 1993.

Coelho, Paulo. *Brida: A Novel (P.S.)*. Harper Perennial, 2009. Kindle edition available.

Collins, Mabel. *Light on the Path & Through the Gates of Gold*. Theosophical Univ. Press, 1997.

Confucius. *The Confucian Analects*. Dover Publications, 1971. Kindle edition available.

Covey, Stephen. *The 7 Habits of Highly Effective People: Powerful Lessons in Personal Change*. Simon & Schuster, 2013. Kindle edition available.

Cummings, E. E. *E. E. Cummings: Complete Poems, 1904-1962*. Harcourt, Brace, Jovanovich, 1972.

De Salzmann, Jeanne. *The Reality of Being: The Fourth Way of Gurdjieff*. Shambhala, 2011. Kindle edition available.

Dostoyevsky, Fyodor. *Notes from the Underground*. Trans. Richard Pevear. Vintage, 1994. Kindle edition available.

Dowman, Keith. *The Flight of the Garuda*. Wisdom Publications, 1994. Kindle edition available.

Emerson, Ralph Waldo. *The Essays of Ralph Waldo Emerson (Collected Works)*. Belknap Press, 1987. Kindle edition available.

Emerson, Ralph Waldo. *The Conduct of Life*. CreateSpace Independent Publishing Platform, 2013. Kindle edition available.

Emerson, Ralph Waldo. *Courage*. Kindle edition available.

Fay, Brian. *Critical Social Science: Liberation and Its Limits*. Cornell Univ Press, 1987.

Feng, Gia Fu and Lao Tsu. *Tao Te Ching*. Vintage, 1989. Kindle edition available.

Fenner, Peter. *Radiant Mind: Awakening Unconditioned Awareness*. Sounds True, 2007. Kindle edition available.

Field Joanna. *A Life of One's Own*. Routledge, 2011. Kindle edition available.

Franck, Frederick. *Messenger Of The Heart: The Book of Angelus Silesius*. World Wisdom, 2005. Kindle edition available.

Freud, Sigmund. *Civilization and Its Discontents*. W. W. Norton & Company, 2010. Kindle edition available

Fromm, Erich. *The Art of Being*. Constable and Company, 1993. Kindle edition available.

Fromm, Erich. *Escape from Freedom*. Holt Paperbacks, 1994. Kindle edition available.

Fromm, Erich. *Man for Himself: An Inquiry into the Psychology of Ethics*. Holt Paperbacks, 1990. Kindle edition available.

Frost, Robert. *The Road Not Taken and Other Poems*. Dover Publications, 1993. Kindle edition available.

Fuller, R. Buckminster. *I Seem to be a Verb*. Bantam Books, 1970.

Gangaji *The Diamond in Your Pocket*. Sounds True, 2007.

Gardner, John. *Grendel*. Vintage, 1989. Kindle edition available.

Gilligan, Stephen *The Courage to Love: Principles and Practices of Self-Relations Psychotherapy*. W. W. Norton & Company, 1997. Kindle edition available.

Hafiz. *A Year with Hafiz*. Trans. Daniel Ladinsky. Penguin Books, 2011. Kindle edition available.

Hafiz. *I Heard God Laughing*. Trans. Daniel Ladinsky. Penguin Books, 2006 Kindle edition available.

Hafiz. *The Gift*. Penguin Compass, 1999. Trans. Daniel Ladinsky. Kindle edition available.

H. H. Dalai Lama *Dzogchen: The Heart Essence of the Great Perfection*. Snow Lion, 2004.

Harvey, Andrew. *A Journey in Ladakh: Encounters with Buddhism*. Mariner Books, 2000. Kindle edition available.

Hawthorne, Nathaniel. *The Scarlet Letter*. Dover Publications, 1994. Kindle edition available.

Helminski, Kabir. *The Knowing Heart: A Sufi Path of Transformation*. Shambhala, 2000. Kindle edition available.

Henley,William. *A Book of Verses*. Nabu Press, 2010. Kindle edition available.

Hesse, Herman. *Demian*. Dover Publications, 2000. Kindle edition available.

Hesse, Herman. *Steppenwolf: A Novel*. Picador, 2002. Kindle edition available.

Higginson, Thomas W. *The works of Epictetus. Consisting of his discourses, in four books, the Enchiridion, and fragments.* Nabu Press, 2010. Kindle edition available.

Hixon, Lex. *Mother of the Buddhas: Meditations on the Prajnaparamita Sutra.* Quest Books, 1993.

Hoffman, Edward. Ed. *The Wisdom of Carl Jung.* Citadel, 2003.

Hollingdale, Reginald J. *Nietzsche: The Man and his Philosophy.* Cambridge University Press, 2001. Kindle edition available.

Hollis, James. *Finding Meaning in the Second Half of Life: How to Finally, Really Grow Up.* Gotham, 2006. Kindle edition available.

Hollis, James. *What Matters Most: Living a More Considered Life.* Gotham, 2009. Kindle edition available.

Hollis, Judi. *Fat is a Family Affair.* Hazelden, 2003. Kindle edition available.

Holmes, Ernest. *This Thing Called You.* Tarcher, 2007. Kindle edition available.

Holy Bible. *New Revised Standard Version.* American Bible Society, 1997.

Horney, Karen. *Neurosis and Human Growth: The Struggle Towards Self-Realization.* W. W. Norton & Company, 1991.

Humphreys, Christian. *The Wisdom of Buddhism.* Routledge, 1995. Kindle edition available.

Huxley, Aldous. *The Perennial Philosophy: An Interpretation of the Great Mystics, East and West.* Harper Perennial Modern Classics, 2009. Kindle edition available.

Johnson, Robert A. *Balancing Heaven and Earth: A Memoir of Visions, Dreams, and Realizations.* HarperOne, 1998. Kindle edition available.

Johnson, Robert A. *He: Understanding Masculine Psychology.* Harper Perennial, 1989. Kindle edition available.

Jung, C. G. *Collected Works of C.G. Jung, Volume 8: The Structure and Dynamics of the Psyche.* Princeton University Press, 1970. Kindle edition available.

Jung, C. G. *Collected Works of C.G. Jung, Volume. 9: Archetypes and the Collective Unconscious.* Princeton University Press, 1970.

Jung, C .G. *Collected Works of C.G. Jung, Volume 13: Alchemical Studies.* Princeton University Press, 1983. Kindle edition available.

Jung, C. G. *Collected Works of C.G. Jung, Volume 17: The Development of Personality.* Princeton University Press, 1981. Kindle edition available.

Jung, C. G. *Memories, Dreams, Reflections.* Vintage, 1989. Kindle edition available.

Katie, Byron. *Loving What Is: Four Questions that Can Change Your Life.* Three Rivers Press, 2003. Kindle edition available.

Kaufmann, Walter. *Faust.* Anchor, 1962. Kindle edition available.

Kazantzakis, Nikos. *Zorba the Greek.* Simon & Schuster, 2014. Kindle edition available.

Khenpo, Nyoshul. *Natural Great Perfection: Dzogchen Teachings and Vajra Songs.* Snow Lion, 2009.

Klein, Jean. *Ease of Being.* Acorn Press, 1986.

Klein, Jean. *I Am*. Non-Duality Press, 2006. Kindle edition available.

Krishnamurti, Jiddu. *Krishnamurti's Journal*. HarperCollins, 1982.

Lao Tsu. *Tao Te Ching*. See Feng, Gia Fu. Vintage, 2012. Kindle edition available.

Le Grice, Keiron. *The Rebirth of the Hero: Mythology as a Guide to Spiritual Transformation*. Muswell Hill Press, 2013. Kindle edition available.

Leunig, Michael. *The Stick and Other Tales of Our Times*. Penguin Global, 2004.

Leunig, Michael. *The Travelling Leunig*. Penguin Books Australia, 1991.

Lowen, Alexander. *Joy: The Surrender to the Body and to Life*. Penguin Books, 1995. Kindle edition available.

MacNulty, W. Kirk. *Freemasonry: Symbols, Secrets, Significance*. Thames & Hudson, 2006.

Maslow, Abraham. *Towards a Psychology of Being*. Sublime Books, 2014. Kindle edition available.

May, Rollo. *Man's Search for Himself*. W. W. Norton & Company, 2009. Kindle edition available.

Merton, Thomas. *No Man is an Island*. Mariner Books, 2002. Kindle edition available.

Mill, John Stuart. *On Liberty*. Dover Publications, 2002. Kindle edition available.

Mill, John Stuart. *Three Essays on Religion*. Cosimo Classics, 2008.

Miller, Henry. *Big Sur and the Oranges of Hieronymous Bosch*. New Directions, 1957. Kindle edition available.

Ming-Dao, Ding. *The Chronicles of Tao*. HarperOne, 1993.

Mirandola, Giovanni Pico della. *Oration On the Dignity of Man*. Gateway Editions, 1996. Kindle edition available.

Moss, Richard. *The Mandala of Being: Discovering the Power of Awareness*. New World Library, 1997. Kindle edition available.

Neumann, Erich. *Depth Psychology and a New Ethic*. Shambhala, 1990.

Nietzsche, Friedrich. *Beyond Good & Evil: Prelude to a Philosophy of the Future*. CreateSpace Independent Publishing Platform, 2014. Kindle edition available.

Nietzsche, Friedrich. *The Untimely Meditations (Thoughts Out of Season Parts I and II)*. Cambridge University Press, 1997. Kindle edition available.

Nietzsche, Friedrich. *Thus Spake Zarathustra: A Book for Everyone and No One*. Trans. R. J. Hollingdale. Penguin Classics, 1961. Kindle edition available.

Nisargadatta Maharaj. *Prior to Consciousness: Talks with Sri Nisargadatta Maharaj*. Acorn Press, 1990.

Nisker, Wes. *Crazy Wisdom*. Ten Speed Press, 1998.

Norbu, Namkhai. *The Crystal and the Way of Light: Sutra, Tantra, and Dzogchen*. Snow Lion, 1999. Kindle edition available.

Olney, Dick. *Walking in Beauty: A Collections of Psychological Insights and Spiritual Wisdom of Dick Olney*. Do Pub Co, 1996.

Pagels, Elaine. *Beyond Belief: The Secret Gospel of Thomas.* Vintage, 2004. Kindle edition available.

Peck, M. Scott. *The Different Drum: Community Making and Peace.* Touchstone, 1998. Kindle edition available.

Peck, M. Scott. *The Road Less Traveled: A New Psychology of Love, Traditional Values and Spiritual Growth.* Touchstone, 2003. Kindle edition available.

Peterson, Jackson. *The Natural Bliss of Being.* CreateSpace Independent Publishing Platform, 2013. Kindle edition available.

Plato. *The Complete Works of Plato [Annotated].* Kindle edition available.

Pope John XXIII. *Pacem in Terris.* America Press, 1963.

Pope, Alexander. *Essay on Man and Other Poems.* Dover Publications, 1994. Kindle edition available.

Prendergast, John J. Ed. *The Sacred Mirror: Nondual Wisdom and Psychotherapy.* Paragon House, 2003. Kindle edition available.

Purton, Campbell. *Person-Centered Therapy: The Focusing-Oriented Approach.* Palgrave Macmillan, 1995. Kindle edition available.

Rand, Ayn. *Atlas Shrugged.* Plume, 1999. Kindle edition available.

Richards, M. C. *The Crossing Point: Selected Talks and Writings.* Wesleyan, 1973. Kindle edition available.

Riley, Henry Thomas. *Three of the Comedies of Terence: Andria, Adelphi and Phormio.* Kessinger Publishing, LLC, 2010.

Robbins, Tom. *Still Life with Woodpecker.* Bantam, 1990. Kindle edition available.

Roberts, Jane. *The Nature of Personal Reality: Specific, Practical Techniques for Solving Everyday Problems and Enriching the Life You Know.* Amber-Allen Publ., 1994. Kindle edition available.

Robeson Jr., Paul. *The Undiscovered Paul Robeson: Quest for Freedom, 1939-1976.* Wiley, 2010. Kindle edition available.

Roerich, Helena. *Leaves of Morya's Garden II: Illumination.* Kessinger Publishing, 2010. Kindle edition available.

Roerich, Helena. *Supermundane: The Inner Life, Book Two.* Agni Yoga Society, 1994.

Rogers, Carl. *On Becoming a Person: A Therapist's View of Psychotherapy.* Mariner Books, 1995. Kindle edition available.

Rogers, Carl. *The Carl Rogers Reader.* Mariner Books, 1989.

Rohr, Richard. *The Naked Now: Learning to See as the Mystics See.* The Crossroad Publishing Company, 2009.

Ruiz, Miguel. *The Four Agreements: A Practical Guide to Personal Freedom.* Amber-Allen Publishing, 1997. Kindle edition available.

Sartre, Jean-Paul. *Existentialism is a Humanism.* Yale University Press, 2007.

Sartre, Jean-Paul. *No Exit and Three Other Plays.* Trans. Stuart Gilbert. Vintage; Reissue edition, 1989.

Schaef, Anne Wilson. *Living in Process: Basic Truths for Living the Path of the Soul.* Ballantine Books, 1998. Kindle edition available.

Schuck, Heather. *The Working Mom Manifesto: How to Stop Hoping for Happiness and Start Creating It.* Voyager Media, 2013.

Scott-Maxwell, Florida. *The Measure of My Days.* Penguin Books, 1979. Kindle edition available.

Shah, Idries. *The Pleasantries of the Incredible Mulla Nasrudin.* Penguin Books, 1993.

Shah, Idries. *The Way of The Sufi.* Penguin Books, 1991.

Shakespeare, William. *Hamlet.* Signet, 1998. Kindle edition available.

Sherwin, Byron L. *Crafting the Soul: Creating Your Life as a Work of Art.* Park Street Press, 1998.

Simon, Simon. *Meeting Yourself Halfway.* Argus Communications, 1974.

Smith, Rodney. *Awakening: S Paradigm Shift of the Heart.* Shambhala, 2014. Kindle edition available.

Smoley, Richard. *Inner Christianity: A Guide to the Esoteric Tradition.* Shambhala Publications, 2002. Kindle edition available.

Spira, Rupert. *Presence: The Art of Peace and Happiness – Volume 1.* Non-Duality Press, 2011. Kindle edition available.

Sri Aurobindo. *Savitri: A Legend and a Symbol.* Sri Aurobindo Ashram Publications, 2010.

Sri Munagala Venkataramiah. *Talks with Ramana Marharshi.* Sri Ramanasramam/India, 2013. Kindle edition available.

Sri Nisargadatta Maharaj. *I am That.* The Acorn Press, 2001.

Swami Nikhilananda *The Bhagavad Gita.* Ramakrishna-Vivekananda Center, 1986. Kindle edition available.

Swami Venkatsesananda *Vasistha's Yoga.* State University of New York Press, 1993. Kindle edition available.

Swami Vivekananda. *Pearls of Wisdom.* Ramakrishna Mission Institute of Culture, 2010.

Tageson, C. William. *Humanistic Psychology: A Synthesis.* Dorsey Press, 1982.

Thomas, Lewis. *The Medusa and the Snail: More Notes of a Biology Watcher.* Penguin Books, 1995.

Thoreau, Henry David. *The Journal of Henry David Thoreau 1837-1861.* NYRB Classics, 2009. Kindle edition available.

Thoreau, Henry David. *Walden and Other Writings.* Modern Library, 2000. Kindle edition available.

Tolle, Eckhart. *A New Earth: Awakening to Your Life's Purpose.* Penguin, 2008. Kindle edition available.

Tolle, Eckhart. *Stillness Speaks.* New World Library, 2003. Kindle edition available.

Tolle, Eckhart. *The Power of Now: A Guide to Spiritual Enlightenment.* Namaste Publishing, 2004. Kindle edition available.

Tolstoy, Leo. *War and Peace.* Vintage, 2008. Kindle edition available.

Trungpa, Chogyam. *Cutting Through Spiritual Materialism.* Shambhala, 2002. Kindle edition available.

Tulku Urgyen Rinpoche *As It Is, Vol. II.* Rangjung Yeshe Publications, 2000. Kindle edition available.

Underhill, Evelyn. *The Spiritual Life*. Morehouse Publishing, 1984. Kindle edition available.

Waite, Arthur. *The Mysteries of Magic: A Digest of the Writings of Eliphas Levi*. Adamant Media Corporation, 2000.

Wallace, Irving. *The Square Pegs: Some Americans Who Dared to Be Different*. Ulan Press, 2012.

Ware, Bronnie. *The Top Five Regrets of the Dying: A Life Transformed by the Dearly Departing*. Hay House, 2012. Kindle edition available.

Wheeler, John. *Awakening to the Natural State*. Non-Duality Press, 2004.

Wheeler, John. *The Light Behind Consciousness*. Non-Duality Press, 2008.

Wheeler, John. *The Wonder of Being*. Non-Duality Press, 2010.

White, John. ed. *What is Enlightenment? Exploring the Goal of the Spiritual Life*. Jeremy P. Tarcher, 1984. Kindle edition available.

Whitman, Walt. *The Complete Poems*. Penguin Classics, 2005. Kindle edition available.

Wiesel, Elie. *From the Kingdom of Memory: Reminiscences*. Schocken, 1995. Kindle edition available.

Wilde, Oscar. *De Profundis: The Ballad of Reading Gaol and Other Writings*. Wordsworth Editions, 1999. Kindle edition available.

Woodman, Marion. *Addicted to Perfection: The Still Unravished Bride: A Psychological Study*. Inner City Books, Canada,1982

Yalom, Ivin D. *Staring at the Sun*. Jossey-Bass, 2009. Kindle edition available.

AUTHOR INDEX

Made in the USA
Middletown, DE
07 November 2019

77913855R00086